THE STUDIO RESET SERIES

BOOK ONE

When the Studio Goes Sideways

A Field Guide for Working Painters

STEVE PUTTRICH

Fairview & Evergreen, LLC

THE STUDIO RESET SERIES

BOOK ONE

When the Studio Goes Sideways

A Field Guide for Working Painters

First in a Series of Books

Built on a Studio Reset Philosophy

Copyright © 2026 Steve Puttrich.

All rights reserved.

Published by Fairview & Evergreen, LLC

Holland, Michigan

www.FairviewFinder.com

The Short Version

I wrote this book. You are welcome to read it, mark it up, fold the corners, argue with it, tape pages of it to your studio wall, and carry it out to your easel in the rain. That is what a field guide is for. If any of it helps you paint more, I will count that as the book doing its job.

What you cannot do is copy it, reprint it, sell it, post it on a website, feed it to a machine that makes more of it, or use it to teach a paid class or workshop without asking me first. Those uses require permission in writing, and I am a friendly correspondent. A short email is usually all it takes.

The difference between the first paragraph and the second is the difference between a reader and a republisher. Readers are welcome here. Republishers need to talk to me first.

The Longer Version (for the Lawyers)

All rights reserved. No part of this book may be reproduced, distributed, or transmitted in any form or by any means, including photocopying, recording, scanning, or other electronic or mechanical methods, without the prior written permission of the publisher, except in the case of brief quotations embodied in critical reviews and certain other non-commercial uses permitted by copyright law.

For permission requests, contact the publisher at the address above, or through www.FairviewFinder.com.

Artificial intelligence notice. No part of this book may be used to train, fine-tune, or otherwise develop any artificial intelligence, machine learning, or large language model system, in whole or in part, without the express written permission of the author. The words in this book were written by a human being in a studio in Michigan, and they belong to him.

Fair use is fine. Short quotations for reviews, critiques, teaching, and honest conversation are welcome. Credit the book and the author, and do not reproduce so much of it that someone could read the whole thing without paying for a copy.

Workshop and classroom use. Instructors who wish to use this book as a text, reference, or handout in a paid workshop or class are encouraged to contact the author for a teaching license. Rates are reasonable. The author is a workshop teacher himself and understands how these things go.

Disclaimers, with a Smile

This book is a field guide based on the author's experience as a working painter and instructor. It is not medical advice, psychological advice, financial advice, legal advice, or marriage advice. If you are dealing with serious mental health issues, please talk to a professional. If you are having trouble with your taxes, talk to an accountant. If you are having trouble with your spouse, this book cannot help, though the author has more than forty years of data suggesting that honest communication and a willingness to be told your painting looks dead are both excellent starting points.

The practices, exercises, and suggestions in this book are offered in good faith. They have worked for the author and for many of the painters he has known and taught. They may or may not work for you. Your studio is your studio. Take what is useful. Leave the rest.

The author makes no promise that reading this book will result in gallery representation, sold paintings, awards, discovery, fame, or financial success. Those are weather. The book is about the practice, not the weather.

Trademarks and Such

Fairview Finder™, Wonder Walking™, Studio Reset™, and the phrase "Design gives clarity. Story gives meaning. Freshness gives life" are trademarks of Fairview & Evergreen, LLC. The Studio Reset series name and philosophy are likewise reserved for future books and teaching materials in the series. Other trademarks and product names mentioned in this book are the property of their respective owners and are used here only in the spirit of honest reference, with no claim of affiliation.

The Seven Ways of Adding Value at Work framework referenced in the Introduction and throughout this book is the intellectual property of

Mark Sanborn, author and speaker (<u>marksanborn.com</u>), and is used here with his gracious permission. The framework has been adapted from its original business and leadership context for application to the working artist's life.

A Note on the Artwork

Any paintings, drawings, photographs, or artwork reproduced in this book are by the author unless otherwise credited. They are included to illustrate principles discussed in the text, and all rights to those images are reserved.

Edition Information

First edition, 2026.

ISBN: 979-8-9955985-1-0

Printed in the United States of America.

Interior designed by **Trinity Czarnik** (czarniktrinity@yahoo.com)

If you found this book useful, tell a painter you know.

Word of mouth is how books find their readers.

If you found it useless, I would still like to hear from you.

The next edition will be better because of it.

Steve

Holland, Michigan

Contents

When the Studio Goes Sideways

A Field Guide for Painters Who Have Hit the Wall

Every working painter I know has had the same morning. You wake up ready to paint. You make the coffee. You walk into the studio. And something is wrong. I can tell you exactly what my version of that morning looked like.

The year was 1980. I was twenty, painfully shy, sitting in Eugene Hall's oil painting class at the American Academy of Art in Chicago. The most beautiful person in the universe was sitting next to me, though I did not yet know she would one day be my wife. What I did know was this: I had been painting for most of my life, and I had just walked into a class that made me feel like I had never painted at all. Every session that first month I stood at the easel and felt, in my chest and my hands, the exact opposite of ready.

Eugene Hall, without knowing he was doing it, was teaching me the first and most important lesson of the book you are holding. Most of the time, the problem is not that you cannot paint. The problem is that the room, the routine, or the person in the chair is not ready. Hall's class had the room right. The routine was built in. What was wrong was me, and the only fix for that was to show up again the next day, and the day after, and the day after that.

Forty-five years later, I still walk into studios where something is wrong, and I still have to diagnose which of the three it is. That is what this book is about.

You cannot name it at first. The room looks the same as yesterday. The tools are in their places, more or less. The panel is waiting. The reference is where you left it. From the outside, everything is in order. But something inside the room is saying no, and you cannot find the source of the no, and within twenty minutes you are standing there feeling like a fraud who has forgotten how to do the thing you have done a thousand times before.

This book is for that morning.

Also, it is for the afternoon when the painting that started strong has turned into mud. For the week when you have not been in the studio because life has been loud and heavy. For the month when you can still paint but cannot remember why you are painting. For the year when the work keeps getting technically better and spiritually quieter, and you are not sure what to do about that.

All of those mornings, afternoons, weeks, months, and years are what I mean by the studio going sideways. It happens to everyone. It is not a sign that you have lost the gift. It is a sign that you are a working painter who has run into one of the recurring problems every working painter eventually runs into. The trouble is both real and common. It is also ordinary. And most of the time, it is fixable.

"Most studio problems are not talent problems. They are room problems, routine problems, mind problems, canvas problems, life problems, and source problems. All of them are workable."

What This Book Is

When the Studio Goes Sideways is a field guide. It is meant to be read once straight through, then kept within reach and opened when you need it. Some chapters you will return to often. Others you will not need until the season changes. Both uses are valid. The book is built for working painters, which means it is built to be used, not just appreciated.

This is also the first book in a series I am calling Studio Reset. The word reset is the heart of the philosophy: the idea that most studio trouble is not fatal, not final, and not a verdict on your ability. It is a signal that something needs to be reset. The room, the routine, the mind, the canvas, the life, or the source. One of them, or several, has drifted out of alignment, and the practice of returning them to working order is what this series is about. Future books in the series will go deeper into specific pieces of the practice: the traveling painter, the teaching artist, the long season, and the daily work of paying attention. For now, this first book covers the whole territory at the level of a field guide, so you have something useful in your hand the next time the studio goes sideways.

There are eight chapters. Each one deals with a different layer of studio trouble, moving from the outside in.

- Chapter One is about the room. Your physical studio. The shop where the work happens.

- Chapter Two is about the routine. How you begin, continue, and stop.

- Chapter Three is about the mind. The fear, perfectionism, and comparison that sit in the chair before you do.

- Chapter Four is about the canvas. Design, story, freshness, and knowing when to stop.

- Chapter Five is about the life. What happens when the days you were planning for do not show up.

- Chapter Six is about the source. The why beneath the how. Wonder, attention, and the part of the work that has nothing to do with craft.

- Chapter Seven is about the special cases. Medium-specific problems, plein air, the teaching artist, post-success stalling, and the other troubles that do not fit neatly into the first six.

- Chapter Eight is the checklists. The whole book folded small, ready to be posted on a wall.

You do not have to read them in order. You probably should, the first time through, because they build on each other. After that, come and go as you need.

The Spine of the Book

If you take nothing else from this book, take three questions. They are the spine of everything else. When the studio goes sideways and you do not know where to begin, ask them in this order.

What is wrong with the room?

What is wrong with the routine?

What is wrong with me today?

Most studio problems live inside one of the three. Usually you can feel which one within thirty seconds of asking, even if you could not name it before. The first question asks whether the physical shop is doing its job. The second asks whether you have a working sequence for getting from walking in the door to making marks. The third asks whether you, the person in the chair, are actually ready to work today, or whether something is in the way.

Most of the book is built around helping you answer those three questions more precisely. The checklists in Chapter Eight are built for days when you need the answers fast. The longer chapters in between are for days when you have time to dig deeper and want to understand why the answers matter.

"When nothing is working, diagnose first. The fix is almost always downstream of knowing what is broken."

Seven Ways of Adding Value

Before we begin, I want to give you one more lens. Not mine. It comes from Mark Sanborn, author and speaker (marksanborn.com), whose work on leadership and service I have found useful in all sorts of places, including the studio. Sanborn teaches that there are exactly seven ways to add value to anything you do. Seven. No more. If you want to improve the quality of your work, your business, your service, or your craft, the improvement has to come from one of these seven directions.

I did not invent this list. I am just passing it along, because once I saw it, I could not stop seeing it everywhere in my own practice. Every good studio day adds value in at least one of these seven ways. Every bad studio day usually fails at all seven. Once you know the list, you can ask it of any painting, any session, any workshop, any week: which of the seven is this adding? If the answer is none, the day did not count. If the answer is one or two, the day was good. If the answer is three or more, the day was great.

Here they are, in the plainest language I can give them.

---

1. Better

Higher quality. The same thing, done more carefully, more skillfully, or with more attention than last time. A painting with a stronger value structure. A thumbnail done with more intent. A cleaner edge where it matters. A more honest mark. Better is the most obvious way to add value and the one every serious painter is already chasing. It is also the hardest to sustain without help from the other six.

2. Faster

Less time to complete. Less time to ship. A workflow that gets you from cold to painting in ten minutes instead of forty. A shutdown routine that clears the studio in five minutes so tomorrow can begin in three. A finishing system that gets paintings out the door in a week instead of six months. Faster is not about rushing the painting. It is about removing the friction around the painting so the painting itself can have all the time it needs.

3. Cheaper

Less expensive to acquire, produce, or maintain. In the studio, this usually means reducing the cost of experimentation. A painter who only works on expensive linen will be afraid to fail. A painter who keeps a stack of cheap panels for studies can fail twenty times before breakfast and learn something from each one. Cheaper, used well, is not about poverty. It is about lowering the emotional price of a mistake.

4. Different

Unique from others. It is about painting what only you can see, from where only you can stand, in the voice only you have. The difference does not come from trying to be different. It comes from being more fully yourself, more specifically, more honestly. The painter who chases trends becomes interchangeable. The painter who paints their own corner of the world cannot be replaced.

5. Less

Doing less of the things that do not work. This one is underrated. Most artists try to add their way out of trouble. More hours. More tools. More subjects. More online presence. More workshops. Sometimes the real improvement is subtraction. Paint fewer subjects and paint them better. Keep fewer tools and use them well. Turn off the notifications. Quit the habits that are eating your attention. Less of the wrong things makes room for more of the right ones.

6. More

Doing more of the things that do work. The mirror of Less. Once you know what is working for you, do it more. More thumbnails. More value studies. More time outside. More silent sessions. More conversations with the honest painter friend who tells you the truth. Whatever is actually feeding the practice, feed it more. Most painters spend their lives doing a little of what works and a lot of what does not. Reverse the ratio and everything changes.

7. Fun

A more enjoyable, remarkable, or memorable experience of doing the work. This is the one most serious painters undervalue, and it may be the most important of the seven. When painting stops being fun, the paintings stop being alive. The joy is part of what the viewer feels in the finished work, and when the joy dies, the paintings die with it. A painter who is enjoying the making produces paintings that feel different from a painter who is grinding. The viewer cannot always name the difference, but they can feel it.

Those are the seven. Better, Faster, Cheaper, Different, Less, More, Fun.

Every day you walk into the studio, you are trying to add one or more of these to the practice. Not all seven at once. That is neither possible nor desirable. But over a working lifetime, a painter who is thoughtfully improving in at least one of these directions at any given time is a painter who keeps growing. A painter who is improving in none of them is stuck, and will stay stuck until something breaks the cycle.

This book is organized around fixing the troubles that keep you from adding value in any of the seven ways. When the room is a mess, you cannot do anything Better, Faster, or More. When the routine is broken, Faster is impossible and Fun is unlikely. When the mind is noisy, Different cannot happen because you are too busy comparing yourself to other painters to find your own voice. When the canvas is failing structurally, no amount of More will save it. When life has taken the tank to empty, Less is the only honest answer. When the source has gone quiet, Fun will not return until you find your way back to wonder.

At the end of every chapter in this book, I will point out which of the seven values that chapter was mostly about. Sometimes it will be obvious. Sometimes it will surprise you. Over the eight chapters, every one of the seven will show up at least once, and most of them will show up more than once. By the time you reach the end of Chapter Eight, the pattern will have been repeated so often that you will start seeing it on your own, without needing me to point it out.

That repetition is deliberate. We painters are in the muscle-memory business. We do not learn by being told a thing once. We learn by doing the thing, watching the thing, hearing the thing, and naming the thing, over and over, until the knowing moves from the head into the hand. The seven ways of adding value work the same way. You do not need to memorize them. You need to meet them often enough, in enough different contexts, that they become a second spine for how you think about your work. Running alongside the three questions in Chapter Eight's triage, the seven will give you another way to think about what you are trying to do when you walk into the studio tomorrow.

"Better, Faster, Cheaper, Different, Less, More, Fun.
Every good studio day adds at least one.
The great ones add several.
The muscle-memory kind adds them without being asked."

How to Read This Book

A few practical notes before we begin.

Each chapter follows the same pattern. A short diagnosis of what goes wrong, followed by ten or more practical approaches, followed by questions to sit with, followed by a closing thought, followed by a short note on which of the seven ways of adding value the chapter was mostly about. The diagnosis sections are meant to earn your trust by naming the trouble plainly. The ten-approach sections are meant to be a buffet, not a prescription. You do not need to do all ten. You need to find the two or three that unlock your particular situation and do those well. The closing thought and the seven-ways note are short on purpose. They give you something to carry with you when you walk out of the chapter and back into the studio.

Different painters will find different things useful. A watercolorist reading the Oil section of Chapter Seven can skip it or skim it. A studio painter reading the plein air section can do the same. The book is built so you can take what applies and leave the rest without missing anything essential. The only chapter I would encourage every reader to sit with, regardless of situation, is Chapter Eight. The checklists are the part you will return to most often.

Mark up the book. Write in the margins. Circle the lines that hit you. Cross out the ones that do not. This is a working book, not a delicate one. It is meant to be used hard and show the wear.

Do not try to apply everything at once. Pick one thing per chapter. Try it for a week. If it helps, keep it. If not, come back for a different one. The painters who get the most out of this book will be the ones who change three or four things over the course of a year, not the ones who try to change thirty things in a week. Three or four things, practiced until they move from the head into the hand, will change your entire year.

Come back. The book will mean different things to you at different points. What you need from Chapter Three today will be different from what you need from it in two years. Chapter Six will hit differently in a hard season than in an easy one. That is why it is a field guide and not a manifesto. It is designed to grow with you.

A Promise

Here is what I can promise you.

If you read this book carefully, try even a handful of the practices in it, and come back to the checklists when the studio goes sideways, you will paint more. You will stall less. The bad days will be shorter. The good days will come more often. The great days, when everything aligns and a painting comes out of you that you did not know you had in you, will still be rare. They always are. But they will arrive more often, and they will arrive because you were at the easel when they came, and you were at the easel because you had built a practice that kept you there through the ordinary days.

I cannot promise that the paintings will sell. I cannot promise that the gallery will call. I cannot promise that you will be discovered, awarded, or remembered. Those things are weather. They are outside the scope of this book and largely outside your control anyway.

What is in your control, and what this book is about, is the daily practice of showing up, doing honest work, and protecting the conditions that make honest work possible. That is a lot. That is almost everything. The rest is weather.

"Do the next clear thing. Then paint."

One more thing before we begin. This book is not a cure. The problems in these pages are not ones you solve and move past. They come back. They evolve. The fear you beat last year will return in a different disguise next year. The room you organized in January will be a mess again by July. The source that is rising in you today will be quiet in some future month, and you will have to find your way back to it again. This is not a failure of the work. It is the nature of the work. A painter is not someone who has solved these problems. A painter is someone who knows how to meet them each time they return.

That is what this book is for. Not to fix you. You do not need fixing. It is to give you a set of tools that will be there, on the wall, in a folder, in the checklist chapter, ready to hand, whenever the studio goes sideways again. Which it will. And which, next time, you will know how to meet.

Now turn the page. We have work to do.

CHAPTER ONE

The Room

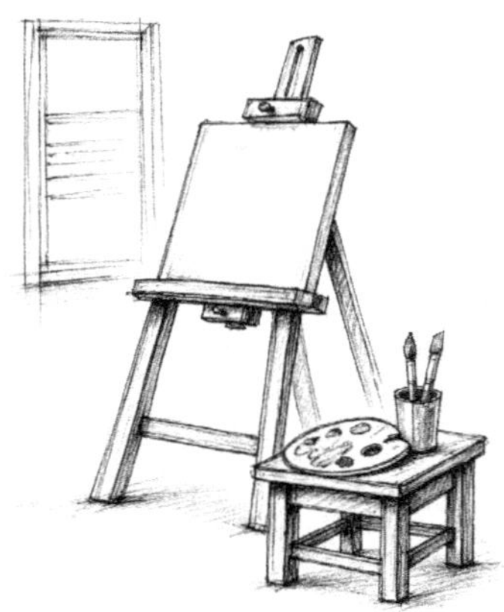

Your Studio Is a Shop, Not a Shrine

There is a particular feeling that comes over an artist when they walk into a studio that is not ready. The body registers it before the mind does. The shoulders tighten. The eyes dart from surface to surface looking for a place to begin, and not finding one. Some part of the brain starts calculating how long it will take just to get to the point where painting is possible. The answer is usually too long. So the artist leaves. Or worse, they stay and push through, and the painting that comes out carries the friction of every cluttered square foot.

I have done this. Every painter I know has done it. We walk into a studio that is supposed to be our sanctuary and we find it full of yesterday's mess, last month's projects, and a decade of things we meant to deal with. We tell ourselves it doesn't matter. Real artists work through mess. Real artists don't care about tidiness.

That is a story we tell ourselves so we don't have to clean up.

The truth is simpler and harder. The room is not a decoration. It is a workspace. It has a job to do. If it cannot do that job, it is costing you every time you walk in. Not in dollars. In decisions. In attention. In the energy that it takes to begin a painting well. You only get so much of that energy in a day, and if you spend half of it fighting your room, you will paint tired before the brush ever touches the canvas.

***"The studio is not a shrine. It is a shop.
Keep it ready for work."***

This chapter is about getting the room right. Not perfect. Not magazine-ready. Right. Functional. Ready to receive you tomorrow morning when you walk in with ten minutes and a good idea.

What Goes Wrong

Before we get to the solutions, let's name the trouble plainly. Here is what a broken studio looks like from the inside.

You cannot find your palette knife. Your brushes are dirty from last time. Paint is scattered on three different surfaces and none of them are the one you meant to paint on. The light is wrong. It was fine when you set it up, but that was a year ago and the seasons have moved on. Your reference is propped against a coffee cup that keeps sliding. There are six unfinished paintings visible from where you stand, and each of them is quietly telling you something you don't want to hear. The smell of yesterday's solvent is still in the air because you forgot to open the window. There is no clean surface to set down a fresh panel. There is nowhere for a wet painting to dry.

This is not one problem. This is fifteen problems, and every one of them is small enough that you could fix it in under two minutes, and large enough that together they make the room feel impossible.

That is the signature of a broken studio. Not one catastrophic failure. A hundred small frictions that add up to a heavy mind.

The Beliefs That Keep the Room Broken

Before you can fix the room, you have to notice what you've been telling yourself about it. These are the stories I hear most often from painters, and I have told most of them myself.

"I'll get organized later. Right now I just need to paint."

Except you don't paint. You stand in the mess and feel defeated, and eventually you leave. The mess prevents the painting. The organization isn't a distraction from the work. It is the work's foundation.

"I work fine in chaos. Real artists don't care about tidiness."

Some do, some don't. But the artists you admire who appear to work in chaos have usually made peace with a very specific kind of chaos. It has a logic only they can see. If you can't find your brushes, that is not artistic chaos. That is just chaos.

"If I had more space, I'd be productive."

Maybe. But I have seen brilliant work made in closets, and I have seen nothing made in spectacular studios. Space is not the variable. Order is.

"I need the perfect setup before I can begin."

This one is the most dangerous because it sounds responsible. It is a permission slip for endless delay. There is no perfect setup. There is a setup that works today, and you can improve it tomorrow.

The Smorgasbord: Ways to Get the Room Right

What follows is not a single method. It is a buffet. Different artists need different things. A watercolorist in a city apartment has different problems than an oil painter in a rural barn. A plein air painter with a garage studio has different needs than a studio portraitist. A teacher who also paints has to manage two jobs in one room. Pick what fits. Leave the rest. Come back to it in six months and try something else.

You do not need to do everything in this chapter. You need to find the three things that unlock your room, and do those well.

1. The Four Zones

The single most useful idea I've ever borrowed for studio setup is the concept of zones. Instead of trying to make one corner do ten jobs, you divide the room by function. Four zones is plenty. Fewer if you have a small space.

Work Zone

This is the easel, the taboret or palette table, and one clear surface within arm's reach. This zone has exactly one job: holding the painting and the tools you are using right now. Nothing else lives here. Not your phone, not your coffee, not the unopened mail. If it is not helping you paint at this moment, it does not belong in the work zone.

Tools Zone

Brushes, medium, knives, rags, solvents, clean-up supplies. Within reach but not on the work surface. A rolling cart is gold for this. So is a pegboard. So is a kitchen drawer organizer. The point is not the container. The point is that every tool has a home, and the home is close enough to reach without breaking rhythm.

Storage Zone

Paint tubes, panels, paper, framing supplies, rarely-used equipment. This is deeper in the room. You don't need to reach it during a session, but you need to find things in under thirty seconds when you do. Shelves, bins, drawers. Labels if you're forgetful. Transparent containers if you're visual.

Drying and Staging Zone

This is the zone most artists skip, and it is the one that breaks the most workflows. You need a place to put a wet painting where it will not be touched, bumped, or stared at. For oil painters, a drying rack or shelf. For watercolorists, a flat board or tilted surface. For plein air painters, a wet panel carrier that can move from car to studio to shelf. If you don't have this zone, finished work accumulates in the work zone and slowly strangles it.

Exercise: Walk into your studio right now with four pieces of masking tape. Label the four zones on the floor or wall. If you don't have a spot for one of them, that is your first problem. Fix that before anything else.

---

2. The One-Surface Rule

If the whole studio is too much to tackle, start smaller. Pick one working surface and declare it sacred. That surface is never used for storage, never used as a junk drop, never used for anything except active painting work.

Everything that lives on it is something you are using in the next hour.

This rule is ridiculous in its simplicity and powerful in its effect. A single clean surface gives you a place to begin. From that place, the rest of the room can stay ugly for a while, and you will still paint.

I have known painters who worked out of garages full of boxes, under the constant threat of their spouse's next yard sale, and still turned out beautiful work. Every one of them had one surface that was clean. That was their island. From that island they could make anything.

Exercise: Right now, identify your one surface. Clear it completely. Wipe it down. Set out only the tools for your next painting. Take a photo of it. That photo is what the surface is supposed to look like when you walk in.

---

3. The Five-Minute Shutdown

Every studio session ends with five minutes of cleanup. Not ten. Not an hour. Five minutes, every single time. Here is what happens in those five minutes:

- Wipe the palette or scrape it flat.
- Clean the brushes you used most.
- Cap the paint tubes that are open.
- Move the wet painting to the drying zone.
- Throw away the rags, the tissues, the trash.
- Reset the work surface so it looks like your photo.

That's it. Five minutes. The reason this works is not magic. It is that the next session begins where this one ended. If you leave a clean surface, you walk in tomorrow to a clean surface. If you leave chaos, you walk in tomorrow to chaos. Your tomorrow-self will either thank you or curse you, and you are the one who decides which.

Richard Schmid had a saying: "Leave your painting area better than you found it, even if you are the only one who was in it." That is the whole discipline in one sentence.

Idea: Put a small, printed sign above your palette. It says, "Five Minutes." When you finish painting, the sign tells you what to do. No decision required. Just the five minutes.

---

4. The Light Problem

Light is the one physical factor that affects your painting more than any other. The light you got when you moved in is usually not the light you need. Here is what matters.

Natural Light

If you have north light, use it. North-facing windows give cool, consistent, directional light that barely changes through the day. This is the traditional studio light for good reason. If you have south, east, or west light, you will need to diffuse it, block direct sun, or paint at specific times of day. Direct sun hitting your palette is not studio light. It is a moving spotlight that will lie to you about every color you mix.

Artificial Light

For consistent work through all hours, invest in daylight-balanced LED panels. The number that matters is color temperature, measured in Kelvin. Aim for bulbs rated between 5000K and 6000K, which approximates the cool directional light of a north-facing window. Also check the Color Rendering Index, or CRI. Look for 90 or above. Cheap bulbs lie about color. Good bulbs do not. Two to four panels, all rated the same, aimed at your palette, your canvas, and if possible your subject or reference. Three points of consistent light is the starting point.

The Kelvin Meter on Your Phone

Here is a trick most painters do not know. There are free Kelvin meter apps that turn your phone into a color temperature reader. Download one. Hold it up to your palette while you paint. The number it reads is the actual color temperature of the light your eyes are working under. This matters more than you think.

If the light reads too warm, below about 4500K, your paintings will drift cool to compensate. You will mix colors that look balanced on the palette and then look blue and sad on a gallery wall under neutral light.

If the light reads too cool, above about 6500K, your paintings will drift warm in the opposite direction. You will mix colors that look right under your studio lights and look yellow and dead everywhere else. The eye compensates for the room automatically, and the compensation ends up baked into the paint.

Brightness follows the same rule. If the light in your studio is too bright, your paintings will come out too dark, because you are adjusting your values to match the glare. Hang those same paintings in a normal room and they will look heavy and muddy. If your studio is too dim, the opposite happens. Your paintings come out too light and chalky, because the shadows you mixed looked convincing in a cave and wash out in actual daylight. Aim for studio light that is bright enough to read comfortably but not so bright you squint.

The Palette and Canvas Rule

Your palette and your canvas must be lit with the same light. If your palette is under a warm kitchen bulb and your canvas is under a cool window, you will mix colors that look right on the palette and wrong on the canvas, and you will never figure out why. Same bulbs, same temperature, same brightness. No exceptions.

Standing Versus Sitting

When I can, I stand. The energy for a painting comes from your feet, travels up through the hips and shoulders, and ends in the brush. You can feel this when you paint standing up and you can feel the lack of it when you paint sitting down. A painting made standing almost always has more life in the marks than a painting made sitting, even when the seated painter is just as skilled.

How you stand matters too. Stand like a fencer. Feet apart, one slightly forward, weight balanced and ready to move. If you are right-handed, put your right foot forward. If you are left-handed, put your left foot forward. This gives you reach, stability, and room to step back without losing your place. It also keeps your shoulders open, which keeps your brushwork loose.

If you have to sit, for health reasons, for long sessions, for detail work on small panels, you can still bring energy to the mark. Sit on the edge of the stool rather than the back of it. Keep your feet flat and slightly apart. Work from the shoulder, not the wrist. And pay deliberate attention to keeping your marks fresh, because a seated painter has to replace with intention the energy a standing painter gets for free. A rubber mat under your feet if you stand, an adjustable stool if you sit, and frequent changes between the two are the sustainable practice. The body you paint in is the body that carries the painting out of you. Take care of it.

---

5. The Grab-and-Go Kit

Keep one kit ready to paint at all times. Not your full studio kit. A compact, self-contained kit with everything you need for a one-hour study. A small box or bag with:

- A limited palette (six to eight tubes).
- Three or four brushes you trust.
- A palette knife.
- A small palette or palette paper.
- Two or three small panels or watercolor sheets.
- A medium and a small container for it.
- A rag or paper towels.
- A Fairview Finder and thumbnail book.

The point of the grab-and-go kit is that it removes setup from the equation. When you have thirty minutes and the whole studio is a mess, you reach for the kit and you paint. When you want to take a walk and paint something small, you grab the kit. When a student asks you to demo, you grab the kit. It becomes your painting reflex, and painting reflexes are what separate artists who make work from artists who talk about making work.

---

*"Thirty minutes of real painting beats
three hours of thinking about painting."*

---

6. The Wall of Inspiration, Used Correctly

Most artists cover their studio walls with inspiration. Reproductions, postcards, quotes, images of paintings they love. This is fine in small doses and deadly in large ones. Here is the rule I have come to: you cannot be inspired by wallpaper. The more things you have pinned up, the less you see any of them.

Pick three. No more. Three images or quotes that genuinely move you, and put them where you will see them while you work. Every few months, swap them out. Let them stay fresh. Let them stay loud.

Eugene Hall, my oil painting teacher at the American Academy of Art, had almost nothing on his studio walls. A few photographs. A couple of small paintings by artists he admired. One or two quotes. That was it. The room was quiet so the work could be loud. I didn't understand that at twenty. I understand it now.

---

7. Ventilation, Comfort, and the Body

Your body is in the room for hours. It deserves better than what most of us give it. A few things to consider:

- **Ventilation.** If you use solvents, you need air movement. A window fan. An open door. A proper ventilation system if you can afford it. Headaches while painting are not a sign of dedication. They are a sign of toxicity.

- **Seating.** A good stool with back support, at the right height for your easel. Adjustable is better than fixed. If you stand, a rubber mat saves your knees and back. These are not luxuries. They are the difference between a three-hour session and a one-hour session.

- **Temperature.** Too cold and your hands get stiff. Too hot and your focus dies. A space heater, a fan, a window. Small investments, large returns.

- **Water.** Keep a water bottle within reach. Dehydration mimics creative block. A glass of water is sometimes the whole fix.

The body is not separate from the painting. The painting comes through the body. Take care of the vessel and the work gets better.

8. The Turn-Around Rule

Unfinished paintings are the single biggest source of quiet guilt in a studio. They stare at you. They remind you of every decision you haven't made, every problem you haven't solved, every piece you meant to finish last month. The cumulative weight of eight unfinished paintings is heavier than the weight of any single one.

Here is the fix: turn them to the wall. All of them. Only the painting you are currently working on faces the room. Every other canvas, panel, or paper gets turned around. You can still get to them. You can still work on them. But they do not watch you while you paint.

This sounds absurd until you try it. The first time I did it, the room felt twenty percent lighter. The paintings were still there. But they were no longer in conversation with me. I could work without their opinion.

Exercise: Turn every unfinished painting in your studio to face the wall. Leave only one facing you. Work only on that one for a week. Notice how different the room feels.

---

9. Setting Up a New Studio: The Returnability Test

If you have just moved, or are setting up a new space for the first time, do not try to perfect it. Try to make it returnable. That is the only question that matters in the first month: can you walk in tomorrow and begin?

Forget the gallery-wall aesthetic. Forget the perfectly organized paint drawers. Forget the vintage taboret you want to buy. The first goal is one working surface, one good light, one place for wet work, one place for tools. That is enough. Everything else you add slowly, as the studio tells you what it needs.

The worst thing you can do in a new studio is unpack everything at once. You will spend weeks putting things in the wrong places and then weeks more moving them. Unpack by frequency of use. What do you reach for first? Set that up. What do you reach for second? Set that up. Leave the rest in boxes until you miss them. Some things you will never miss, and those are the things you didn't need.

Your first goal is not beauty. It is returnability. Can you walk in tomorrow and begin?

---

10. The Studio Rules, Written and Posted

Somewhere in your studio, tape a piece of paper to the wall. On it, write three to five rules you have made for yourself. Not aspirational rules. Actual rules. Things you will do every session without fail. Here are a few examples from my own studio over the years, written at different times for different reasons:

Phone in the other room.

Start with a thumbnail. No exceptions.

Step back every ten minutes.

Stop before it goes dull.

Five minutes of cleanup at the end.

Your rules will be different from mine. They should be. The point is not the specific rules. The point is that you have written them down and they are visible. When you walk into the studio and feel the usual confusion, the paper tells you what to do. No willpower required. Just follow the paper.

Questions to Sit With

Before you move on to the next chapter, take a few minutes with these. You don't have to answer them in writing. But let them settle.

- When I walk into my studio tomorrow morning, what is the first thing I will see?

- Of the four zones (work, tools, storage, drying), which one is working well for me? Which one is missing?

- What is one surface I could make sacred starting today?

- What am I keeping in my studio that I do not need and cannot bring myself to throw away? Why?

- If a painter I admire walked into my studio tomorrow, what would I wish were different?

- Is my light helping me, or have I just gotten used to it?

- What would my five-minute shutdown look like if I started it tonight?

A Closing Thought

The room is the container. It does not make the painting, but it holds the painting. Hold it well and the work gets easier. Hold it poorly and the work gets heavier. Most artists underestimate how much of their creative struggle is actually a room problem in disguise.

You do not need a beautiful studio. You need a working one. A room that does its job quietly, so your mind is free to do the harder, stranger, more wonderful work of making something from nothing.

Clean one surface. Set one good light. Give your tools a home. Put a sign that says "Five Minutes" above your palette. Turn the unfinished paintings to the wall. Pick three rules and tape them up.

Then paint.

Of the seven ways of adding value, this chapter was mostly about **Faster** and **Less.** A working room removes friction, which makes you faster to begin every time you walk in. It also asks you to do less of the wrong things: less clutter, less visual noise, less hunting for tools you should have been able to find in ten seconds. Faster and Less are quiet gifts. Nobody sees them in the finished painting, but the painter who has them feels the difference in every session.

"Do the next clear thing. Then paint."

CHAPTER TWO

The Routine

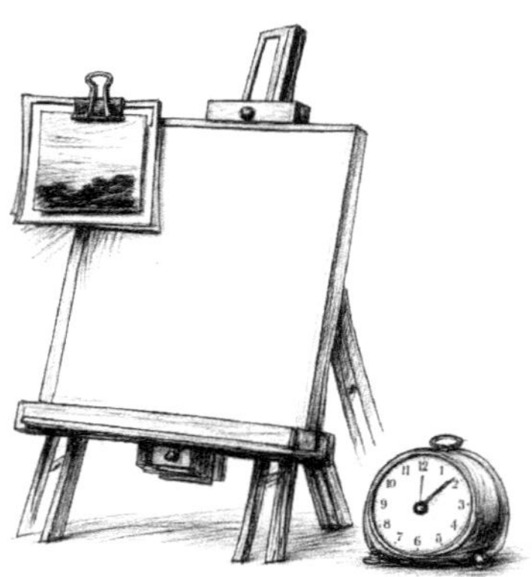

How to Begin, How to Continue, How to Stop

You walk into a clean studio. The room is ready. The light is good. The palette is set. You have the whole morning.

And you sit there for forty-five minutes, unable to begin.

You scroll through your reference photos. You pick one. You change your mind. You pick another. You make a cup of coffee. You pick the first one again. You stare at the blank panel. The morning that was going to be yours is now half-gone, and you have not made a single mark.

This is not a room problem. The room did its job. This is a routine problem. And of all the things that stall painters, this one is the quietest and the most expensive.

Routine is the word artists tend to resist. It sounds mechanical. It sounds like the opposite of art. We like to imagine we paint best when we are free, spontaneous, following the muse wherever she leads. And sometimes we do. But most of the time, the muse does not show up on her own. She shows up because we built a door she could walk through.

That door is routine. It is the sequence of small, repeatable actions that takes you from walking into the studio to putting paint on the surface.

When the door is built, you walk through it without thinking. When it is not, you stand in the hallway for forty-five minutes trying to remember how to begin.

"A good painting requires about forty consequential decisions. If you make them in random order, you will contradict yourself by decision twelve."

This chapter is about building that door. Not one way. Many ways. Different painters need different sequences, different warm-ups, different permission slips. The goal is not to copy my routine. The goal is to find one that fits your hand and use it long enough that it becomes invisible.

What Goes Wrong

Workflow trouble has a particular flavor. Room trouble makes you tired before you begin. Routine trouble makes you anxious once you have begun. It feels like standing in front of a canvas without knowing what step comes next, or like three hours in realizing the composition was wrong from the start, or like finishing a painting and not being sure whether you finished it or just stopped.

Here is what broken workflow looks like from the inside.

You sit down and do not know what to paint. You open your reference folder and look at sixty photos. None of them feel right. You keep looking. When you finally pick one, you are already tired and the painting has not started. You skip the thumbnail because you want to get to the good part. You start directly on the canvas with color, without a value plan. Twenty minutes later you realize the composition is wrong, but you have already committed so you push through. At some point you lose track of the big shapes and start painting details on a structure that was never sound. You work for four hours and never step back. When you do step back, you do not recognize what you made. You keep going, hoping to save it. You overwork. You give up. You scrape. You begin the next one the same way.

Every step in that paragraph is a missing piece of routine. Not one big failure. Eight small ones, each of which could have been prevented by a simple decision made earlier.

The Beliefs That Keep the Routine Broken

"I paint intuitively. Planning kills spontaneity."

The painters whose work looks most intuitive almost always plan more than you think. Sargent made careful drawings before his most dashing watercolors. Sorolla did thumbnails for his beach scenes. The spontaneity you admire is built on a foundation you cannot see. Planning does not kill spontaneity. It protects it.

"I'll figure it out as I go."

Sometimes you will. More often you will figure out, three hours in, that you should have figured it out three hours earlier. Figuring it out as you go is a fine strategy when the stakes are low and the painting is small. It is a terrible strategy on a large canvas with a complicated subject.

"Thumbnails are a waste of time."

A two-inch thumbnail takes ninety seconds. A wrong composition on a sixteen-by-twenty panel takes four hours. The math is not subtle.

"Starting over means failure."

No. Starting over means you noticed something wasn't working and had the courage to fix it. The real failure is pushing through a broken foundation because your ego got attached to the first fifteen minutes.

The Smorgasbord: Ways to Build a Better Routine

What follows is a buffet of routines, rituals, and sequences. Some you will love. Some will not fit your temperament. Some will work for a year and then stop working, and you will replace them with something else. All of that is normal. The goal is not to find the one true routine. The goal is to stop winging it.

1. The Six-Step Entry Sequence

This is the simplest and most useful routine I know. Six steps, always in the same order, every time you begin a painting. It takes about fifteen minutes if you move briskly. It prevents roughly eighty percent of the problems you would otherwise discover three hours in.

1. **Choose one reference.** Not three. Not a stack you will decide between. One. Commit.

2. **Write the story in one sentence.** "This painting is about ____." If you cannot finish the sentence, you are not ready to paint. Go back to the reference.

3. **Do one thumbnail.** Two inches. Ninety seconds. Three values. No color. Just the big shapes and where they sit on the rectangle.

4. **Set the three values.** On your thumbnail, mark light, middle, and dark. You are looking for a readable value structure before you touch paint. If the thumbnail doesn't read at arm's length, redo it.

5. **Mix the big color families.** Before you touch the canvas, mix the dominant color pools: sky family, land family, focal family. Pre-mixing is not cheating. It is preparation.

6. **Begin with the largest shapes.** Cover the canvas in the first five minutes. No details. No drawing lines. Just the big masses of value and color, roughly placed.

If you do nothing else different, do these six steps. The painters I know who adopted this sequence almost universally reported the same thing: not that they painted better right away, but that they began more easily and wasted less. The wasted-less part is the gift. You make more paintings because each one doesn't cost you three hours of recovery.

---

2. The Warm-Up Study

Musicians do not walk onstage and immediately play the concerto. They warm up. They play scales. They get the fingers moving, the ears open, the mind settled. Painters mostly skip this step, and then wonder why the first twenty minutes of every session are stiff and the first painting of the day is the worst one.

A warm-up study is a small, low-stakes painting you do before the painting. Five by seven. Fifteen minutes. No ambition. Its only job is to get your hand and eye moving together.

Some artists warm up with a value study of something simple: a piece of fruit, a coffee cup, the corner of the room. Others do a quick color note from memory. Others copy a small section of a master painting. Richard Schmid talked about the importance of what he called alla prima studies as daily practice. Kevin Macpherson does small starts. Edgar Payne treated plein air as a warm-up for studio work. All of them were building the same muscle: the one that takes you from cold to ready without demanding you make a masterpiece first.

Idea: Keep a stack of five-by-seven panels permanently next to your easel. Every session begins with one. Paint it in fifteen minutes. Then begin the real work.

---

3. The One-Sentence Intent

Before you paint, write one sentence. Just one. "This painting is about the way the afternoon light pools in the north pasture." Or "This painting is about the loneliness of an empty road." Or "This painting is about the shape of the big oak against the hill."

That sentence is your compass for the next three hours. When you get lost mid-painting (and you will), come back to the sentence. Ask: is what I am doing right now serving this sentence? If yes, continue. If no, stop.

The sentence is not poetry. It is navigation. Some artists write it on the edge of the panel in pencil where only they can see it. Others keep a small notebook on the taboret and write it there. One painter I know writes it on a Post-it and sticks it to her easel. The method does not matter. The sentence matters.

> **"If you can't say what the painting is about in one sentence, the painting doesn't know either."**

---

4. The Step-Back Rhythm

The painting you see with your nose six inches from the canvas is not the painting anyone else will see. Everyone else will see it from eight feet. If you only paint at six inches, you are designing for an audience that does not exist.

What works is to step back, on a schedule, whether you feel like it or not. Here are a few rhythms to try:

- **Every ten minutes.** Set a timer. When it rings, step back ten feet. Look. Then reset the timer.

- **Every color mix.** Every time you mix a new pool of color, step back before you apply it.

- **Every fifteen strokes.** Count your brushstrokes. Step back on the fifteenth. Crude but effective.

- **Every cup of coffee.** Use the bathroom, refill your water, walk around the room. Then look at the painting.

Different rhythms work for different painters. What matters is that you have one. The painting that feels almost-done at six inches is often badly broken at eight feet, and if you never step back, you will not find out until it is too late.

Exercise: Today, set a timer for ten minutes and step back every time it rings. Keep a tally of how many times you were genuinely surprised by what you saw. The surprises are the reason for the rhythm.

---

5. Pre-Decisions: Choosing Before You Enter

Decision fatigue is the quiet killer of studio time. Every small choice costs you a little bit of the finite decision-making energy you brought in that day. By the time you get to the choices that actually matter, you are running on empty.

The fix is to make the small decisions the night before. Or the morning before. Or on the way to the studio. Anywhere but in the studio itself. Here are decisions you can move upstream:

- Which reference will I paint tomorrow?

- What size and format?

- What is the one-sentence intent?

- What colors will I put on my palette?

- How long do I plan to work?

- What will I do first if I get stuck?

If you answer these six questions before you walk into the studio, you walk in ready. You begin immediately. You save the finite decision energy for the actual painting, where it belongs. This is not micromanagement. It is preparation. Every chef does it. Every surgeon does it. Every carpenter does it. We are the only ones who keep pretending it's beneath us.

---

6. The Stopping Protocol

Most painters have no plan for how to stop. They paint until something makes them stop: exhaustion, frustration, hunger, disgust. None of those are good stopping points. By the time exhaustion arrives, you have probably already overworked the painting by thirty minutes.

Here are several ways to build a real stopping protocol.

The Timer

Set a timer for ninety minutes, or two hours, or whatever you know to be your best working window. When it rings, stop. Not stop-when-I-reach-a-natural-stopping-point. Stop. Put the brush down. Step back. Look. If you have more to do, write down what. Come back tomorrow. Constraints produce clarity. Open-ended sessions produce overworked paintings.

The Three-Touch Rule

Once you believe the painting is almost done, give yourself three more touches. Three brushstrokes or three small decisions. Then you are done, whether or not it is perfect. This is a cure for the fiddling that destroys more good paintings than any other single cause.

The Photograph

Take a photo of the painting on your phone. Look at it on the small screen. The small screen lies about details but tells the truth about design. If the painting reads on the phone, it is probably done. If you are still trying to fix small things, you are fiddling.

The Walk-Away

Put the painting face-to-the-wall. Leave the studio. Do something else for an hour. Come back and look at it fresh. The first glance will tell you what the painting needs, if anything. Usually the answer is: nothing. You were about to fix things that were not broken.

"Stop before the painting goes dull."

---

7. The Cleanup-As-Transition

Chapter One talked about the five-minute shutdown as a way to keep the room working. Giving yourself a mental transition is the other reason. The cleanup ritual marks the end of the session the way a closing prayer marks the end of a meeting. It gives your mind permission to stop painting.

Without the cleanup, the painting session just sort of trails off. You stop at the canvas, walk away, and the painting follows you out of the room. You think about it all evening. You second-guess choices you made at the easel. You fall asleep trying to fix it in your head.

With the cleanup, the session ends on purpose. You wipe the palette. You clean the brushes. You put the tools back. You turn the painting to the wall or to the drying rack. You leave the studio with empty hands. The mental residue lifts. The next session can begin fresh.

This is not mysticism. It is just how human minds work. Endings matter. Build one into your routine.

8. The Weekly Rhythm

A good routine is not just about the session. Different days should serve different purposes. Trying to make every studio day a breakthrough day is like trying to run a marathon every morning. You will burn out fast.

Here is one possible weekly rhythm. Yours will be different. Use it as a starting point.

- **Monday: Studio Reset Day.** Clean, organize, prep surfaces, review last week's work. Low creative demand. High logistical value.

- **Tuesday: Study Day.** Small warm-ups, color notes, master copies, value studies. Low stakes, high learning.

- **Wednesday and Thursday: Production Days.** Real paintings. Your best hours and your freshest mind.

- **Friday: Review Day.** Photograph finished work. Update records. Frame what needs framing. Plan the next week.

- **Saturday: Exploration Day.** Plein air, experiments, new techniques, play. No agenda.

- **Sunday: Rest.** Actually rest. Not just not-paint. Rest.

Again, this is one example. You may have a day job and get two studio days a week. You may be retired and have seven. The point is not the specific schedule. The point is that not every day is the same day. Give each day a job. Give yourself permission to do that job and nothing more.

---

9. The Notebook Beside the Easel

Keep a notebook within reach of your easel. Not for the finished insights. For the raw ones. When you notice something mid-painting ("I always mix my skies too warm"), write it down. When you see a mistake you keep making ("I lose the big shape once I start adding detail"), write it down. When you find something that works ("pre-mixing three piles of green saves me twenty minutes"), write it down.

The notebook is not a journal. It is a workbench. Over months, it becomes the most honest mirror of your own practice that exists. You will see patterns. You will catch yourself making the same mistake twelve times and finally get angry enough to fix it.

Eugene Hall told his students to keep what he called a "lessons book." Just a cheap spiral notebook. Every class, write down one thing you learned. Not a deep reflection. Just one line. At the end of a year, you have three hundred and sixty-five lines of honest practice. That book, he said, is worth more than any textbook you will ever buy.

Exercise: Buy a cheap notebook today. Put it next to your easel. Tomorrow, write one line in it. The day after, write another. Do not worry about being insightful. Just be honest.

---

10. The Permission to Start Badly

This is the last and in some ways the most important piece of routine. Give yourself permission to begin badly. Not as a consolation prize. As a working strategy.

The best painters I know all start their paintings in a way that would make a beginner nervous. The first fifteen minutes look like a mess. Thin, sketchy, loose, seemingly chaotic. They are not making the painting in the first fifteen minutes. They are making a platform the painting can stand on. The platform is allowed to be ugly. It just has to be right.

Beginners want every brushstroke to be good from the first mark. That is impossible, and the pursuit of it is what makes the first twenty minutes of their paintings stiff and anxious and bad. The professionals know they are going to make a mess. They have made peace with it. They go in confident because they know the mess is part of the process, not a failure of it.

Build this permission into your routine. Say it out loud at the beginning of each session if you need to. "The first fifteen minutes are going to look bad, and that is the plan." It sounds silly. It works.

For years I have used Christmas cards as a way to practice starting. For six years or so I painted them in watercolor. Then one November I switched to little oil paintings on primed watercolor paper. The routine stayed the same. A seven by ten inch sheet of watercolor paper is cut from full sheets. A four by six window is taped off on the bottom of each sheet. Green Frog taped out, I then prime the window with gesso, to protect the paper fibers from the oils. Six sheets taped to a board at a time. Ten to fifteen minutes per card. At the end of an hour, six small paintings are done and drying.

People have asked me over the years why I do not just paint one good one and print the rest. I understand the question. It is a reasonable question. The Christmas cards are not really about the cards. They are about the doing of the thing, six times in an hour, about 130 cards in a season, loose and fresh and without permission to be precious.

That repetition builds muscle memory that carries into the rest of my painting year. The blessing is not in the card I give away. The blessing is in the thing it teaches my hand during the making. It is training disguised as generosity. If I could give you only one assignment for the next month, it would be this: find your own version of the Christmas card. Six small things in an hour. Then do it again next week. Keep starting. Keep starting badly. Keep going.

"Start smaller than your fear. Start uglier than your pride."

Questions to Sit With

Before you move on to the next chapter, sit with a few of these. Pick the ones that sting the most. Those are the ones worth your attention.

- What is the first thing I do when I walk into the studio? Is it a decision or a habit?

- Do I have a repeatable sequence for beginning a painting, or do I rebuild it every time?

- When was the last time I did a thumbnail before a painting? What would change if I did one today?

- Do I know why I am painting this particular subject, or did I just default to it?

- How do I stop a painting? Do I stop on purpose, or do I stop because I ran out of patience?

- Do I step back on a schedule, or only when I happen to remember?

- What decision could I move upstream so I don't have to make it in the studio?

- If I kept a one-line notebook of lessons learned, what would this week's entry say?

A Closing Thought

Routine is the part of painting that nobody celebrates and everybody needs. It is unglamorous. It is repetitive. It is exactly the kind of thing that makes artistic people uncomfortable, because we like to believe we are above such things.

We are not. The artists I most admire are the most routined people I have ever met. They have entry rituals and exit rituals. They have warm-ups and stopping protocols. They have weekly rhythms and daily checklists. They have notebooks beside their easels and one-sentence intents taped to their palettes. They look, from the outside, like people following rules.

From the inside, they are people who have freed themselves from having to decide a hundred small things every day, so that all their remaining creative energy can go where it matters: into the painting.

Routine is not the enemy of art. It is the friend that carries art's luggage so art can walk lightly. Build the routine. Then paint.

Of the seven ways of adding value, this chapter was mostly about **Faster** and **Better.** A working routine gets you from cold to painting in minutes instead of hours, which is Faster in the truest sense. And the small disciplines inside the routine, the thumbnail, the one-sentence intent, the step-back rhythm, are all about making the next painting Better than the last one. Routine is the engine that powers both. The painters who resist it are usually the ones paying the highest price in lost mornings.

"The muse visits painters who are already at work."

The Mind

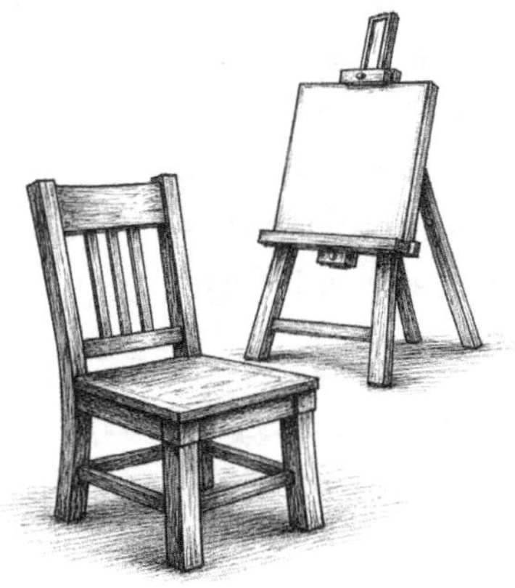

CHAPTER THREE

When the Studio Becomes a Courtroom

The room is clean. The routine is in place. You have your reference, your thumbnail, your one-sentence intent. By every practical measure, you are ready.

And you cannot pick up the brush.

There is a weight sitting on your chest that has nothing to do with the painting. It is a mix of things that are hard to name individually: some fear, some shame, some comparison, some old voices you thought you had put down, some new voices you picked up on the internet this morning. Together they are telling you that this painting matters too much, that you cannot afford to fail, that you should be further along than you are, that everyone else is doing better than you, that if this one goes badly it will mean something about who you are.

None of that is true. All of it feels true.

This is the chapter where we deal with the part of painting that has nothing to do with paint. The room can be perfect and the routine can be airtight, and you can still stand in front of a blank panel with a heavy heart and an empty hand. This is not a character flaw. This is what it feels like to be a painter with a mind.

Every painter I admire has felt this. Sargent walked away from portraits for years after Madame X. Sorolla pushed through bouts of discouragement that would have broken lesser men. Andrew Wyeth talked openly about the dread that hit him at the start of every new painting. The mind that makes art is the same mind that doubts the art it makes. You cannot have one without the other. What you can do is learn to work with the doubt instead of being ruled by it.

"The mind that makes art is the same mind that doubts the art it makes. You cannot have one without the other."

"The mind that makes art is the same mind that doubts the art it makes. You cannot have one without the other."

This chapter is not therapy. I am not qualified to give that and you do not need it from a book about painting. This chapter is about working strategies. Practical ways to turn down the volume on the voices that stop you, so you can get back to the work.

What Goes Wrong

The mind has many ways of stopping you from painting. Most of them feel like reasons. They feel like they are telling you something true about the situation. They are not. They are habits of thought that have hardened into walls.

Here are the five most common walls, and what they feel like from the inside.

Fear

Fear is the quietest of the walls because it rarely announces itself as fear. It disguises itself as responsible caution. It tells you the reference isn't quite right yet. It tells you the surface needs more preparation. It tells you you should organize your brushes first. It tells you you're not in the right mood. It tells you anything except the truth, which is that you are afraid to make a mark you cannot take back.

Perfectionism

Perfectionism sounds like high standards and feels like paralysis. It is the belief that if you cannot do it well, you should not do it at all. It is what makes you abandon paintings at the first sign of trouble, because a ruined painting feels worse than an unfinished one. It is a thief with excellent manners.

Comparison

Comparison is the wall social media built. You look at another painter's finished, photographed, filtered, carefully-posted work and you compare it to your own half-done, unphotographed, in-progress mess. You lose every time. You were always going to lose, because you were comparing the wrong things.

Shame

Shame is the accumulated weight of every painting you meant to finish and didn't, every session you meant to show up for and skipped, every goal you set and missed. It is the voice that says, quietly, that you are not the painter you told people you were. It is wrong, but it is persuasive.

The Referendum

The most dangerous belief in the studio is that this painting reveals whether you are good enough. The Referendum belief turns every session into a verdict. Win or lose. Worthy or unworthy. It is exhausting, and completely made up. No painting reveals anything about your worth. A painting reveals what you noticed, what you tried, what you learned. Nothing more. Nothing less.

The Beliefs That Keep the Mind Stuck

"If I were really talented, this would not be so hard."

Talent does not make painting easier. It makes it possible. The painters with the most talent often struggle the most, because they can see the gap between what they want and what they can do more clearly than anyone else. The struggle is not a sign you lack talent. It is a sign you are paying attention.

"I should be past this by now."

No. You should be exactly where you are. "Should" is a word we use to punish ourselves for being human on a human timeline. Every painter at every level deals with some version of this. The forty-year veteran is still struggling, just with different problems. You do not outgrow the struggle. You grow into a more interesting version of it.

"If I can't do it well, I'd rather not start."

This one is the most expensive of all, because it sounds reasonable. It is not. The painters who get good are the ones who are willing to make bad paintings for years. That is the price. There is no other path. The alternative to a bad painting is not a good painting. It is no painting at all.

"Everyone else seems to produce so much more than I do."

Everyone else is showing you their highlight reel. You are comparing your full life, including the dark days and the sick days and the discouraged days, to their best-curated moments. It is not a fair fight. Stop having it.

The Smorgasbord: Ways to Work With the Mind Instead of Against It

What follows is not a set of mindset hacks. Those do not work for long. What follows is a collection of practical strategies, habits, and small acts of resistance that I and the painters I know have found useful when the mind is the main obstacle. Different ones will speak to different temperaments. Take what helps. Leave the rest.

The goal is not to eliminate the fear, the comparison, the perfectionism, the shame. Those are not going to disappear. The goal is to stop letting them drive. You can be afraid and still paint. You can compare and still paint. You can feel ashamed and still paint. Painting through the feeling is what makes the feeling weaker over time. Avoiding it is what makes it stronger.

---

1. Lower the Stakes on Purpose

When the mind is loud, the single most useful thing you can do is make the next painting small. Not because small paintings are better. Because small paintings are lower stakes, and lower stakes quiet the voices that only speak when they think something important is on the line.

Go to a five-by-seven. Or a four-by-six. Or a three-by-five card. Make something you could not possibly ruin in any meaningful way. Use cheap materials if the good ones are making you nervous. Use paper instead of panel. Use a medium you are less attached to.

The mind quiets down when it realizes nothing important is happening. Once it quiets down, you can paint. Once you can paint, you are a painter again. And once you are a painter again, the stakes can slowly come back up.

Exercise: For the next week, paint only on surfaces smaller than six by eight inches. No big canvases. No important pieces. Just small, low-stakes studies. Notice what changes in your mind by day four.

2. The Twenty-Minute Timer

Set a timer for twenty minutes. Commit to painting for those twenty minutes, and only those twenty minutes. No judgment during the timer. No stepping back to evaluate. No deciding if it's working. Just paint until the timer rings.

The timer does two things. First, it creates a container that contains the fear. You are not committing to making a great painting. You are committing to twenty minutes. That is a promise you can keep. Second, it separates the making from the judging. During the twenty minutes, you are in production. After the twenty minutes, you can evaluate if you want. Or you can set another timer. Or you can stop.

I have used this for years. It is the most reliable trick I know for getting past the wall of not-starting. The mind cannot maintain its anxiety about a twenty-minute commitment. It is simply too short a window for the stakes to feel real.

***"The mind cannot maintain its anxiety about a
twenty-minute commitment."***

---

3. Name the Fear Out Loud

When you notice you are avoiding the studio, or standing in front of
the canvas unable to begin, try this: say out loud what you are afraid of.
Specifically. In real words. Not "I'm blocked." That is not what it is. Say
something more honest.

> *"I'm afraid this painting will prove I've lost it."*
>
> *"I'm afraid the gallery will be disappointed with my next delivery."*
>
> *"I'm afraid I am not the painter I tell people I am."*
>
> *"I'm afraid that after all this time, I still can't draw trees."*

Fear shrinks when you speak it plainly. Not because speaking it makes
it untrue, but because speaking it makes it manageable. The formless
dread that was sitting on your chest becomes a specific, named fear.
Specific things are workable. Formless dread is not.

You do not have to share the fear with anyone. You just have to say it
out loud in an empty studio. The walls will not judge you. The fear will
be smaller by the time the sentence is done.

I knew an artist once who was struggling with two traveling companions
called Fear and Procrastination. He kept waiting for the perfect moment to
paint. The perfect weather. The perfect scene. The mountaintop workshop.
The friend to go out with. The day when the schedule would finally settle.

He never found that perfect moment. Fear and Procrastination took
over his life. Even when a good day did come up, he could not bring
himself to use it.

That artist was me. The year was 2003. My day job had me painting
less and less, and at some point I looked up and realized I had been
carrying those two companions for longer than I wanted to admit.
I did not say the word "fear" out loud for a long time, because I had
been raised to think fear was something serious men did not have. But
one day I finally did. I said it in the kitchen, to my wife Bobbie. I told
her I was afraid I was losing it. Afraid that if I did not paint more, I
would not be able to paint at all.

Bobbie, as she has done a thousand times since, refused to pretend the problem was not real. She also refused to let it stay the size it had become. She said: we are going to do something about this. We discovered the plein air movement together that same year. We invested in good gear so there would be no excuse. We signed up for workshops. We made it so easy to paint that we would have had to actively refuse in order to not paint.

Here is the thing I did not understand until I said the fear out loud. I had been trying to fight against fear. You cannot fight against fear directly. Fear is not a thing you can hit. It is a weather. You fight for something instead. For beauty. For adventure. For the painting you want to make tomorrow. When you are fighting for something, fear is still there in the room, but it is no longer driving. It is sitting in the back seat complaining, and you can ignore it, because you are busy.

That is what naming the fear out loud did for me. Not because the naming was magic. Because once the fear had a name, I could stop arguing with it and start arguing for the other thing.

---

4. The Ugly Painting on Purpose

Once a month, make a deliberately bad painting. Not a bad painting you tried to make good. A bad painting you set out to make bad. Ugly colors. Weird composition. Things that should never happen in a serious painting.

This sounds childish. It is not. It is a muscle-memory exercise for the nervous system. You are teaching yourself that making a bad painting does not hurt. You survive it. Nothing bad happens. The sky does not fall. Your identity does not collapse. You made a bad painting, and you are still you.

Once your body knows this at a visceral level, the fear of making a bad painting accidentally loses most of its power. You already made a bad one on purpose last week. You proved to yourself it was survivable. Now when the next painting threatens to be bad, you can shrug and keep going.

Idea: Keep a stack of deliberately ugly paintings in a drawer. When you get too precious about a piece, take one out and look at it. Remember that you survived making it. The current painting cannot possibly be worse than that one, and you are still here.

---

5. The Private Practice

Make some work that no one will ever see. Not for Instagram. Not for the gallery. Not for the newsletter. Not even for the sketchbook you show students. Actually private. Work that exists for you and nobody else.

Artists forget this is possible. We have become conditioned to treat every painting as potential content. Every stroke feels like it might need to be photographed. Every finished piece is evaluated for sharing. This is a recent development in the history of painting, and it is doing something quietly destructive to our ability to experiment.

Private practice restores the part of painting that existed before anyone was watching. The part where you tried something strange just because you wondered what would happen. The part where failure had no audience and therefore no cost. The part where you painted the way you painted when you were eleven years old and nobody had told you yet that it mattered.

Keep a private sketchbook. Or a stack of small panels in a closed box. Or a folder on your computer no one else ever sees. Make work there regularly. The private practice is where your voice gets room to breathe. The public work is where it eventually shows up, stronger for having been protected.

"Your voice grows where no one is watching.
Then it shows up where they are."

---

6. The Comparison Fast

If comparison is your particular wall, try this: go on a comparison fast. Thirty days without looking at other painters' work. No Instagram. No

Pinterest. No gallery websites. No juried show announcements. No peer feedback groups. None of it.

This will feel radical. You will feel like you are missing something. You are not. You are missing the noise. What you keep is the signal: your own eye, your own subject, your own instinct, your own voice.

At the end of thirty days, come back to looking at other work and notice how differently it lands. You will be able to admire without losing yourself. You will be able to learn without measuring. You will remember what it felt like to paint before the comparison machine was running in the background all day.

Some painters do this for a weekend and feel the relief. Others do it for a month. A few do it permanently, making a rule to only look at other artists' work in museums, in books, or in person. They are usually the ones making the most distinctive work.

Exercise: Try a three-day comparison fast. Delete the apps from your phone for seventy-two hours. Notice what you think about instead. Notice what you paint instead.

---

7. The Peer, Not the Platform

Social media is not community. It is a broadcast tower. The comments and likes feel like connection, but they are not. Real community is different. Real community is one or two painters you trust enough to show unfinished work to. The ones who will tell you the truth because they love you and love the work.

Find one. Cultivate it. Protect it. A single honest painter friend is worth more than ten thousand followers. They see you on a normal day, not a curated day. They know the painting you're struggling with, not just the one you finished. They can tell you when you're being too hard on yourself, and when you're not being hard enough.

If you do not have that person yet, look for them. Workshops are one of the best places to meet them. Plein air events. Small local paint groups. The painters you meet in person, face to face, easel to easel, are the ones most likely to become the real ones. The online relationships can be wonderful, but the most important ones are almost always grounded in shared rooms and shared days.

Eugene Hall used to say that the most important person in a painter's life, after their own discipline, was the honest friend. Not the encouraging friend. The honest one. The one who would tell you when a painting was weak and mean it, and tell you when it was strong and mean that too.

---

8. The Finish-It-Anyway Rule

When a painting goes sideways, the temptation is to abandon it. Scrape it. Set it aside. Tell yourself you'll come back to it. You almost never come back to it. It joins the pile of unfinished pieces that slowly become a monument to unfinished-ness.

Instead, finish it anyway. Finish it badly. Push it to some conclusion, even a bad one. The act of finishing, regardless of quality, builds a muscle that abandoning destroys. Every finished painting, even an ugly one, strengthens your confidence that you can see things through. Every abandoned painting weakens that confidence, even if you do not notice the erosion.

This is about training your nervous system to believe that finishing is the default. When finishing is the default, you will occasionally finish a painting that surprises you. When abandoning is the default, you will mostly have piles.

Exercise: Look at your studio right now. Find one unfinished painting you have been avoiding. Give yourself thirty minutes to finish it badly. Not to save it. To finish it. Put the final mark down. Sign it if it deserves signing. Dispose of it if it does not. Experience the feeling of completion, even on a piece that did not earn it by quality.

---

9. Separate the Making From the Judging

The mind has two modes. Making mode and judging mode. They cannot run at the same time. When you are making, you are committed, immersed, exploratory. When you are judging, you are standing back, measuring, evaluating. Both modes are necessary. Both are useful. But when they try to run simultaneously, neither works well.

Most artists lose sessions because they try to make and judge at the same time. They put a stroke down and immediately criticize it. They mix a color and immediately doubt it. They start a painting and immediately evaluate whether the whole thing will be any good. This is the fastest known way to paralyze yourself.

Separate the modes on purpose. When you are painting, paint. Do not evaluate. Do not second-guess. Trust the plan you made in the routine and execute. When the timer rings, or when you reach a natural stopping point, switch modes. Step back. Evaluate. Decide what needs to change. Then switch back to making mode and execute the change.

Some painters find it helpful to physically move between modes. Make at the easel. Judge from across the room. Never judge while holding a brush. The physical separation reinforces the mental one.

"When you are making, make. When you are judging, judge. Never try to do both at once."

---

10. The Long View

Finally, and most importantly, learn to take the long view. Not the view of the next painting. The view of the next decade.

In ten years, the painting you are struggling with today will not matter. You will barely remember it. What will matter is whether you kept painting through the struggle. Whether you showed up. Whether you built the habit. Whether you were still at the easel five years from now, and ten years from now, and twenty. That is what makes a painter. Not any individual painting. The accumulated weight of thousands of sessions, most of them unremarkable, many of them frustrating, a few of them magical.

When the mind is telling you this painting is a disaster and it means something terrible about who you are, the long view is the best answer. This painting is one of thousands. It is a single data point in a life. Its job is not to be brilliant. Its job is to exist, so the next one has something to stand on.

Sergei Bongart, the Russian-American painter who taught generations of students in Santa Monica and Idaho, used to say that the only thing separating the artists from the would-be artists was mileage. Just mileage. The ones who painted enough paintings eventually became painters. The ones who waited until they were good enough to start never started at all. The mileage was the whole secret. There was no other secret.

Take the long view. This painting is not the test. The next ten thousand paintings are the test, and you pass that test one brushstroke at a time, today, whether or not today feels like it matters.

"Mileage is the whole secret. There is no other secret."

Questions to Sit With

These are heavier than the questions in earlier chapters. Do not rush them. Pick one. Sit with it for a day. Pick another tomorrow.

- What am I afraid of when I avoid the studio? Can I say it in one sentence?

- Whose voice am I hearing when I criticize my own work? Is it mine, or did I borrow it from someone?

- When I compare myself to other painters, what exactly am I comparing? Is the comparison fair?

- Do I have one honest friend I can show unfinished work to? If not, where might I find one?

- When was the last time I finished a painting I thought was bad? How did it feel afterward?

- What would change if I believed that every painting was just one of ten thousand, and none of them had to be perfect?

- Am I making and judging at the same time? What would it look like to separate them?

- If I took the long view, the ten-year view, would I be more afraid, or less?

A Closing Thought

The mind is the part of painting that nobody told you about when you started. You thought it was going to be about drawing, and color, and learning the medium. Those things matter, and they take years. But the mind is the thing that turns out to be the longest lesson of all, because the mind goes with you into every session, every painting, every decade.

You will never completely silence the fear. You will never completely stop comparing. You will never completely outgrow the voice that tells you you should be further along. What you can do is learn to keep painting while those voices are talking. You can paint through them. And every time you do, they get a little quieter, and the painting gets a little stronger, and you get a little more free.

The studio is not a courtroom. You are not on trial. Nobody is grading this. The painting in front of you is not going to reveal whether you are good enough, because that was never the question. The question was always whether you would show up, do the work, and come back tomorrow. You already know how to answer that one. You have been answering it every time you opened this book.

Paint the next small thing. Then the next one. Let the accumulation do its quiet work. The mind will follow, eventually. It always does.

Of the seven ways of adding value, this chapter was mostly about **Fun** and **Less.** Painting stopped being fun when comparison, perfectionism, and the Referendum moved into the studio and took the good chairs. The work in this chapter is about asking them to leave, so the joy that was there before they arrived can come back. That joy is Fun, in the deep sense Sanborn meant it. And it only returns when you do Less of the things that were drowning it out. The quiet room and the quieter mind are the same room in the end.

**"You are not your last painting.
You are your next honest decision."**

**"You'll never feel ready because ready isn't a feeling,
It's a decision"**

CHAPTER FOUR

The Canvas

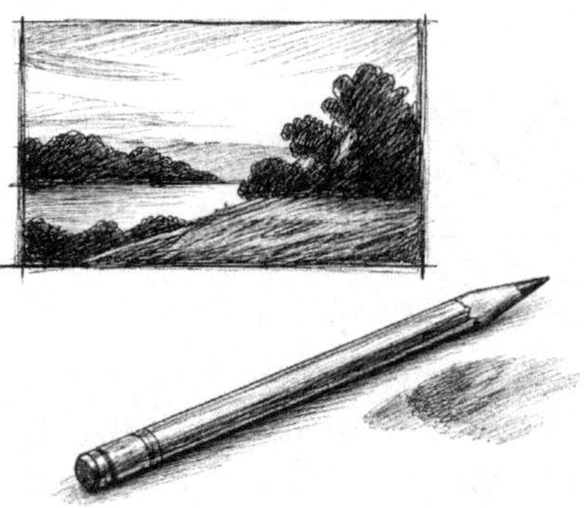

Design Gives Clarity. Story Gives Meaning.
Freshness Gives Life.

Sometimes the studio feels wrong because the painting is wrong.

Not morally wrong. Structurally wrong. You walk in, the room is ready, the routine is humming, the mind is relatively quiet, and still something feels off. You make marks and they do not land. You mix colors and they come out muddy. You step back and the painting looks busy but says nothing. You cannot tell what is broken, only that something is.

This is the most misdiagnosed problem in a painter's life. We feel the trouble and assume it is about us. We are tired, or lazy, or not talented enough, or going through a phase. We reach for psychological explanations when the real answer is sitting right there on the canvas, perfectly visible, if we knew where to look.

A lot of artist discouragement is not emotional first. It is design pain misdiagnosed as a life problem. The painting is failing for structural reasons, and the structural failure feels like a personal failure because we have not learned to separate the two.

This chapter is about the structural side. The canvas itself. What is happening inside the rectangle. The four things a painting needs in order to work, and the ten approaches that will help you deliver them.

"Design gives clarity. Story gives meaning. Freshness gives life."

These three lines are not a slogan. They are a diagnostic tool. When a painting is failing, one or more of them is missing. Find which one, fix that one, and most of the time the painting comes back to life. This chapter is built around them, with a fourth element added at the end: knowing when to stop.

What Goes Wrong

Here is what a painting in trouble looks like from the inside.

The composition feels static or trapped. Everything gets equal attention. There is no clear focal point, and nothing in the image tells the viewer where to look first. The values are all middle tones, so the whole painting reads flat at a squint. The color is muddy or chalky or overstated. The edges are all the same hardness, so nothing advances or recedes. You have rendered the photograph instead of interpreting it. You started with details and never found the structure. The marks are timid. The painting looks worked-on but not alive.

Any one of these is fixable. Several of them together create the sinking feeling that the whole painting is wrong and should be scraped. Sometimes that is the right call. Usually it is not. Usually you are one or two good decisions away from a painting that works.

The question is knowing which decisions those are. That is what this chapter will train you to see.

The Beliefs That Keep the Canvas Stuck

"I just need better drawing skills."

Maybe. But most of the time the drawing is not the problem. The design is. You can draw perfectly and still make a dead painting if the design is wrong. You can draw loosely and make a great painting if the design is right. Drawing is a skill. Design is a decision. Most artists are trying to solve design problems with more skill, and it does not work.

"If I get the color right, the painting will work."

Color is what everyone notices, and few understand. It is also what almost nobody understands. Color does not save a painting. It decorates one. If the values are wrong and the shapes are wrong, no amount of beautiful color will fix it. The color that looks so good on the palette looks muddy on the painting because the structure underneath it is broken.

"I need to paint exactly what I see."

No. You need to paint what matters about what you see. There is a difference. The reference gives you everything at once, with equal weight. The painting has to choose. If you paint everything, you say nothing. If you paint only what matters, you tell the viewer what you saw.

"More detail will save it."

Detail rarely saves a painting. It usually finishes it off. When the big relationships are wrong, adding small ones just distributes the wrongness more evenly. The painting gets busier without getting better. Detail is a reward you earn after the structure is sound. Not before.

The Smorgasbord: Ten Ways to Make the Canvas Sing

What follows is organized around the three words: Design, Story, Freshness. Plus stopping. These are not techniques. They are ways of thinking about the painting that open up better decisions. Each one is a lens. Pick the lens that matches the problem you are looking at.

---

1. The Three-Value Squint Test

This is the single most useful design tool I know, and it costs nothing. Stand six feet back from your painting and squint until your eyes are almost closed. When you squint, your eyes stop seeing detail and start seeing value masses. Everything reduces to light, middle, and dark.

Now ask yourself: can I see three clear value shapes? Is one of them clearly dominant? Is there a clear focal point where the highest contrast lives? If the answer is yes to all three, the design is working. If the answer is no to any of them, you have found the problem, and you do not have to look any further.

A painting that reads at a squint will almost always read at full strength. A painting that does not read at a squint cannot be saved by anything you do at full strength. Values are not one element among many. They are the structural foundation. When they work, everything else has a chance. When they do not, nothing else matters.

Exercise: Squint at your current painting right now. Can you identify the three main value shapes in under five seconds? If not, the design is broken. Go back to the thumbnail and fix it there, not at full scale.

***"If the painting does not read at a squint,
stop adding and start simplifying."***

---

2. The Hierarchy of Shapes

Every good painting has a hierarchy. Some shapes are big. Some are medium. Some are little. The big ones carry the structure. The medium ones carry the story. The little ones carry the accents. They do not carry the painting. They finish it.

The mistake most artists make is treating all shapes as equal. They give as much attention to a tiny flower in the foreground as they do to the massive sky behind it. The result is a painting where everything competes and nothing wins. The viewer's eye has nowhere to rest.

Here's what I do to make it work, establish the hierarchy deliberately. Before you paint, decide: what is the biggest shape? What is the second biggest? What is the smallest important shape? Paint them in that order. Big first. Medium next. Small last. Never the other way around.

Edgar Payne had a set of composition principles he drilled into his students: the steelyard, the group mass, the tunnel, the silhouette, and a handful of others. Each was just a different way of organizing shapes into a clear hierarchy. He did not care which one you used. He cared that you used one. A painting with a clear shape hierarchy can survive almost any other problem. A painting without one cannot be rescued by any amount of skill.

Idea: Before you start your next painting, write down three numbers on a scrap of paper: the approximate percentage of the canvas taken up by your largest shape, your second-largest shape, and your third-largest shape. If the numbers are roughly equal, you have a design problem before you begin.

---

3. The One-Sentence Story

We touched on this in Chapter Two. Here it comes back, because it belongs to the canvas as much as to the routine. The one-sentence story is the beating heart of Story with a capital S. It is what tells the painting what it is about.

Without a story, a painting is a visual inventory. A list of objects rendered carefully. With a story, the same objects become a statement. The difference is not what you put in. It is what you emphasize, what you subdue, and what you leave out. And you cannot emphasize, subdue, or leave out until you know what the painting is about.

The story does not have to be literary. It does not have to be a narrative. It can be as simple as "the way the late light turns the grass orange." Or "the loneliness of an empty dock." Or "the softness of the air after rain." What matters is that the sentence gives you a compass. When you are mid-painting and unsure whether to include a detail, you ask: does this detail serve the sentence? If yes, include it. If no, leave it out.

Most paintings fail because they have no sentence. The artist painted whatever was in the reference, and the reference had no opinion. A painting without an opinion is a painting with nothing to say, and viewers can feel that immediately even if they cannot name why.

"A painting without an opinion is a painting with nothing to say."

---

4. The Focal Point and the Sacrifice

A focal point is the place in the painting where the viewer's eye is meant to land first. It is usually where the highest contrast lives, often where the sharpest edges are, sometimes where the brightest color sings. It is the destination the painting leads the eye toward.

Most failing paintings have no focal point because the artist wanted everything to be interesting. That is the wrong goal. You do not want everything to be interesting. You want one thing to be interesting and the rest to serve it. The rest is the supporting cast. The focal point is the lead actor.

The hardest part of establishing a focal point is the sacrifice. To make one area sing, every other area has to be quieter. That means subduing colors you love, softening edges you spent time on, throwing detail away from places that feel important to you. This is where most artists flinch. They cannot bear to make anything quiet, so they make everything loud, and nothing ends up heard.

Richard Schmid used to talk about painting in terms of what to sacrifice. He would ask his students, what are you willing to lose to save the whole painting? The answer is usually: quite a lot. A few beautiful passages must die so the painting can live. That is the deal. You cannot keep everything and also have a focal point.

Exercise: Look at your current painting. Identify the focal point. Now identify the three areas that should be quieter than they currently are. Make them quieter. See what happens to the focal point.

---

5. The Value Plan Before the Color Plan

Color is seductive. It is what makes us fall in love with a subject and rush to the easel. It is also what trips up more paintings than any other single element. Most painters mix color too early and hope values will work themselves out. They rarely do not.

The cure is to solve values first, always, before you think about color. On the thumbnail, before anything else, work out your three values. Where is the light? Where is the middle? Where is the dark? How much of the canvas does each one occupy? Which one dominates?

Once the values are solved in black and white, color becomes almost easy. You are no longer using color to establish structure. You are using color to add temperature, emotion, and specificity on top of a structure that already works. The color decisions get easier because the hard work has already been done.

This is why the old masters painted grisaille underpaintings. This is why the Russian school drilled students on value studies for years before letting them touch color. This is why every serious painting instructor I have ever studied with has said some version of the same thing: get the values right and color will follow. Ignore the values and no amount of color will save you.

Idea: For the next five paintings, do a value study in graphite or charcoal before you mix a single color. Five minutes each. See how many of your color problems disappear.

---

6. Edges: The Hidden Language

Edges are the most overlooked element in painting, and they may be the most important after value. An edge is the boundary between two shapes. It can be hard, medium, or soft. It can be lost entirely. And the hardness of every edge sends a message to the viewer about what matters and what does not.

The rule is simple: hard edges go where you want attention, soft edges go where you do not, and lost edges go where shapes merge into one another for rest. A painting where every edge is the same hardness reads as flat and unresolved, because the eye has no way to prioritize. A painting with a full range of edges reads as dimensional and confident, because the eye is being directed.

Most beginning painters treat every edge the same because the reference photo shows every edge the same. The camera cannot prioritize. You can. You must. Every edge is a decision. Every edge is a chance to tell the viewer something about what matters.

John Singer Sargent was a master of edges. If you look closely at his portraits, almost nothing is fully rendered. The face has a few hard edges where they count. The clothes dissolve into the background. The hands are often suggested more than drawn. He knew that the power of a painting was not in rendering everything clearly. It was in deciding what to render clearly and what to let go.

"Every edge is a decision.
Every decision is a chance to tell the viewer what matters."

---

7. Big Shapes to Small, Never the Other Way

The order in which you paint matters as much as what you paint. The rule is simple and almost always ignored: start with the biggest shapes and work toward the smallest. Never begin with details and try to build outward. You will lose the structure every time.

Here is the sequence that almost never fails. Cover the canvas in the first five minutes with the biggest masses of value and color. Do not draw lines. Do not worry about accuracy. Just get the big relationships down. Then, in the next thirty minutes, refine those masses into more specific shapes. Then, in the next thirty, start distinguishing the medium shapes. Only in the final stretch do you allow yourself the smallest shapes, the accents, the details.

This is the opposite of how most people naturally want to paint. Most people want to start with the eye of the dog, the pupil of the eye, the highlight on the pupil. This is intuitive and wrong. The painting built outward from a detail has no structural foundation. When the detail is surrounded, it looks isolated and stiff. The painting built inward from the big masses has a foundation that supports every detail you eventually add.

Sorolla used to block in huge areas of color within minutes of starting. From a distance the canvas looked like an abstract painting for the first hour. Only later did the specific figures, water, and sand emerge. He was building the foundation before the house.

Exercise: On your next painting, give yourself exactly five minutes to cover the entire canvas with the big shapes. No details allowed. Step back. Does the painting already read, at a squint, without any small information? If yes, you have built the right foundation. If no, fix the big shapes before touching anything smaller.

---

8. Interpretation, Not Rendering

The reference photo is a tool, not a boss. Most artists treat it the other way around. They treat the photograph as the truth and the painting as an attempt to copy that truth. This is why so many paintings made from photographs feel lifeless. They are copies of something that was already a copy.

Interpretation means deciding what the photograph got wrong and fixing it. The camera flattens values, overstates details in shadow, weakens color at distance, and gives equal weight to things that should have a hierarchy. Your job is to correct all of this. The photograph shows you what was there. The painting shows what mattered.

This is the single biggest shift between a painter who renders and a painter who interprets. The renderer asks, what does the photograph look like? The interpreter asks, what did I feel when I saw it? What was the real subject? What should be louder than the photograph made it? What should be quieter? What should disappear entirely? The painting that results is not more accurate. It is more true.

Every great landscape painter I have studied worked this way. Payne exaggerated the drama of his mountains. Cezanne flattened his Provencal hills. Sargent simplified his landscapes into big masses of tone. None of them were copying. All of them were interpreting. The painting was a report from the eye and the heart, not from the lens.

Eugene Hall used to say, "The reference photo is a starting point, not a finish line." He would sometimes turn the photo upside down partway through a painting so his students would stop copying it. He wanted them to paint what they remembered, not what they could see.

---

9. Freshness: Stopping Before the Painting Dies

There is a stage in some of my paintings I only half-jokingly call the homicide stage. It is the moment past the point where the painting was done, when I keep adding paint anyway, and the painting that was alive twenty minutes ago is now lying on the ground bleeding out, and I am still holding the weapon, wondering why I cannot see what I am doing.

One spring a few years ago I was working on a close-in piece of the bridal wreath in our backyard. The bush had been blooming for a week and I had already done one study from farther away. This second attempt was tighter and more ambitious and by the second hour I had lost the thread entirely. The patterning of the blossoms had turned against me. Every mark I made was making it worse. I could feel it going wrong but I could not find my way back out.

I called in the only reinforcement I had. Bobbie walked over, looked at it, and without flinching told me what was wrong with the pattern structure. Once she had said it, I could see it. I could not have seen it on my own because I was too deep in the killing. She bailed me out of that painting the way she has bailed me out of many others, with the clarity that only comes from not being the one who made the mess.

The lesson is not that you need a Bobbie. Not everyone has one. The lesson is that most overworking is invisible to the person doing it, and what helps is to introduce some form of outside eye before you cross the line. A second person, if you have one. A photograph on your phone. A walk around the block. Anything that lets you look at the painting the way a stranger would look at it, before you put in the last fifteen minutes that take it from done to dead.

Freshness is the hardest of the three to define and the easiest to recognize when it is missing. A fresh painting feels alive. The marks feel confident. The color feels direct. The whole image feels like it was made by someone who knew what they wanted and did it with commitment. A dead painting feels the opposite: labored, uncertain, overworked, fussy. The difference is not technical skill. It is knowing when to stop.

Most painters overwork. Not a few. Most. Myself included. The urge to fix just one more thing, to refine just one more area, to push just a little further, is the urge that kills more good paintings than any other single cause. By the time you can see the problem, the damage is already done.

The honest answer is to stop earlier than you think you should. Much earlier. If you think the painting is ninety percent done, it is probably done. If you think it is done, you are probably already five minutes past done. The last fifteen minutes you almost always regret.

Here are a few tricks for catching the stopping point before you pass it. Take a photograph of the painting every fifteen minutes during the final hour. Look at them afterward. You will almost always see that one of the earlier photos was stronger than the finished version. That earlier photo is where you should have stopped. Next time, stop there.

Another trick: when you believe you are almost done, put the painting face-to-the-wall and walk away for ten minutes. When you come back, the painting will look different. Your eye will be fresh. You will see immediately what it needs, which is almost always: nothing. You were about to fix things that did not need fixing.

"If you think the painting is done,
you are probably already five minutes past done."

---

10. The Three Questions at the End

When you think a painting is finished, run it through three questions before you sign it. These three questions catch most of the things you will regret later.

Does it read at a squint?

Squint from across the room. Can you still see the three main value shapes? Is there still a clear focal point? Does the painting still have its structure? If yes, the design held up through the detail work. If no, you have overworked it and you need to restate the big shapes before you stop.

Does it say one thing clearly?

Can you walk someone else up to the painting and have them understand, without you explaining, what it is about? If the painting's story is not clear to a viewer in the first few seconds, you have a story problem. You do not have to fix it right now. But you should notice it, so next time you catch it earlier.

Does it feel alive?

This is the hardest question to answer honestly. Look at the brushwork. Look at the edges. Look at the color. Does the painting feel like someone made it with confidence, or does it feel like someone labored over it? If the former, stop. If the latter, you are probably past the point where additional work will help. Put it away and try again tomorrow on a fresh surface.

Three questions. This ritual at the end of a painting will save you from signing work you regret and will teach your eye, over time, to recognize the difference between finished and overworked before you cross the line.

Questions to Sit With

These are the most technical questions in the book so far. Use them as a diagnostic tool on your current paintings, not as an abstract exercise.

- When I squint at my most recent painting, can I see three clear value shapes in under five seconds?

- Do I have a hierarchy of shape sizes, or is everything roughly equal?

- Can I state, in one sentence, what my current painting is about? If so, does every part of the painting serve that sentence?

- Where is the focal point? What am I willing to sacrifice to protect it?

- Am I solving values before color, or am I mixing color first and hoping values will work out?

- Are my edges varied, or are they all the same hardness?

- Am I painting big shapes to small, or starting with details?

- Am I interpreting my reference, or copying it?

- When was the last time I stopped a painting earlier than I wanted to? What happened?

A Closing Thought

The canvas is where everything comes together. The clean room and the good routine and the quieted mind all lead here, to the rectangle in front of you and the decisions you make inside it. If the canvas is failing, no other part of the studio can fix it. If the canvas is working, every other part of the studio feels lighter.

Design gives clarity. Without clarity, the viewer does not know where to look. Story gives meaning. Without meaning, the viewer has no reason to care. Freshness gives life. Without life, the viewer feels the labor but not the love. These three together are what make a painting work. Miss any one of them and you will feel the painting go flat before you can name why.

But here is the good news. All three are learnable. None of them require special talent. They require attention, sequence, and the willingness to make hard decisions about what to keep and what to sacrifice. You do not have to be gifted to paint well. You have to be clear, honest, and disciplined about the decisions that matter. The rest is practice.

When your next painting feels wrong, do not reach for a psychological explanation first. Reach for the diagnostic tools in this chapter. Squint. Check the hierarchy. Say the sentence. Look for the focal point. Ask what you have sacrificed. Most of the time, the answer is sitting right there on the canvas, and the fix is one or two good decisions away.

Design, Story, Freshness. Then stop. That is the whole craft in four words. Everything else is detail.

Of the seven ways of adding value, this chapter was mostly about **Better** and **Different.** Better is the obvious one. Every painter wants the next painting to be stronger than the last, and the tools in this chapter are the ones that make it so. Different is the quieter sibling. When you stop copying your reference and start interpreting it, the painting becomes yours in a way a copied painting can never be. Better and Different work together. Better without Different produces skilled work that could have been made by anyone. Different without Better produces personal work that does not quite hold together. You need both, and this chapter was about making them fit in the same rectangle.

"You do not have to be gifted to paint well.
You have to be clear, honest, and disciplined about
the decisions that matter."

The Life

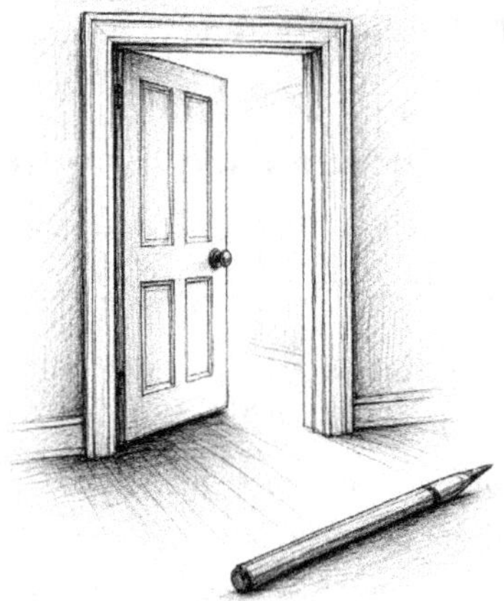

CHAPTER FIVE

Painting Through the Days You Weren't Planning For

It is Friday evening. The week has been full. You meant to paint three times and each time something happened: a sick kid, a long meeting, a car that needed a tire, a friend who needed an ear. You kept telling yourself there was still time. Now it is dark, the studio door is closed, and you are standing in the kitchen holding a cup of tea that is slightly too cold, making a quiet deal with yourself about next week.

Next week you will paint. Next week things will settle. Next week you will have the time and the energy and the focus you did not have this week.

You have made this deal before. You will probably make it again. And you already know, somewhere under the fatigue, that next week is going to be another full week, and the week after that, and the week after that. Life does not settle. Life just keeps arriving, wave after wave, and at some point you either find a way to paint in the middle of it or you stop being a painter.

This chapter is not about discipline. It is not about willpower. It is not about pushing through. I have tried all three of those and they fail more often than they work, especially in the seasons that need them most.

This chapter is about something older and gentler: the practice of staying a painter when the days you were planning for do not show up, and the days you were not planning for do.

***"Some seasons are for painting.
Some seasons are for staying a painter."***

Most of the time, when artists talk about life getting in the way, they mean the ordinary invasions: the full schedule, the tired body, the phone that will not stop, the responsibilities that come before the studio door. These are real. They deserve serious thought, and this chapter gives them that. But underneath those, there is a second layer that is even more important: the hard seasons. Illness. Grief. Caregiving. Moves. Money trouble. The years when the tank simply cannot be filled to where it used to be.

Both layers need different things from you, and learning which one you are in is part of the work.

What Goes Wrong

Life invading the studio has a particular texture. It is not dramatic. It is cumulative. A hundred small concessions, each one reasonable on its own, that add up over weeks and months to a painter who has stopped painting without ever deciding to stop.

Here is what it looks like from the inside. You walk past the studio door five times in a day and every time you think about going in. Something always stops you. A text. A load of laundry. A task you remembered. You finally make it in at three in the afternoon and discover you only have forty-five minutes before you have to pick someone up. You cannot start anything in forty-five minutes, you tell yourself, so you organize your brushes instead. By the time the brushes are organized, it is time to leave. You close the door behind you with the satisfying feeling of having been in the studio, and also the suspicion that you did not paint anything.

Or it looks like this. You sit down in the studio in the morning, ready to begin, and before you pick up the brush you check your phone for just one second. Thirty minutes later you surface from an argument in the comments of a post you did not even mean to read, and the good morning energy is gone. You paint, but the paintings are flat, because you painted them with the mind of someone still in the argument.

Or it looks like this. You have been caring for an aging parent for six months. Every day is a crisis. You come home exhausted and cannot imagine painting, so you do not. You tell yourself this season will pass and then you will get back to it. The season does pass. And when it does, you discover that the habit of not-painting has taken root, and starting again is harder than it should be, because six months of absence is a long time for a practice to go cold.

Each of these is a different problem. Each of them needs a different answer. Lumping them all together as "life getting in the way" hides the distinctions that would help you.

The Beliefs That Keep Life in Charge

"When things settle down, I'll get back to painting."

They will not settle down. Not in the way you are imagining. There will be easier weeks and harder weeks, better seasons and worse ones, but the expanse of uninterrupted time you are waiting for is not coming. It does not exist anywhere in adult life. The painters who eventually make work are the ones who stopped waiting for the settle and started painting inside the storm.

"I can't paint unless I have a full day."

Yes you can. You have never needed a full day. A full day is a nice luxury. A half day is a real blessing. An hour is plenty. Thirty minutes is enough. You have done it before. You are doing it this moment, in your head, as you read this. The belief that you need a full day is a wall you built yourself, and the wall is what is keeping you out of the studio, not the schedule.

"I should be able to push through."

Not always. Sometimes the right move is to push through. Sometimes the right move is to rest. The maturity is knowing the difference, and it is not a character flaw to need rest. The flaw is refusing to tell the truth about which one you are in today. The body is not lazy when it asks for sleep. It is telling you something true about what is possible in the next two hours.

"Other people need me more than my work does."

Sometimes that is true and you should go to them. Sometimes it is not true and you are using it as a reason to avoid a harder thing. The painters I know who have kept a practice through decades of family life and caregiving and crisis all learned the same hard lesson: if you never take your own work seriously, nobody else will either. Protecting one half hour a day for the studio is not selfish. It is the minimum you need to stay the person they love.

The Smorgasbord: Ten Ways to Paint Inside a Life

What follows is a collection of practices, permissions, and accommodations that I and the painters I know have used to keep working through ordinary weeks, hard weeks, and the occasional impossible year. They are not presented in order of importance. Pick what fits the season you are actually in, not the season you wish you were in.

---

1. Maintenance Mode

This is the single most important idea in this chapter, and it is the one most artists refuse to accept. There are two modes for a painting practice: production mode and maintenance mode. Most of us assume we are always supposed to be in production mode, and we treat maintenance mode as failure. That is backwards. Maintenance mode is how production mode stays alive during the seasons when production is not possible.

Production mode is what you do when life is cooperating. Studio days are long. Energy is high. You are finishing paintings, shipping work, making progress. This is the season most artists are thinking about when they plan their year.

Maintenance mode is what you do when life is not cooperating. You might not be finishing anything. You might not even be making finished paintings. What you are doing is protecting the habit. Cleaning brushes. Priming panels. Making one study a week. Reorganizing the palette. Spending ten minutes looking at a subject without painting it. Reading a book about painting. Thinking about color. Stretching a canvas. Any of these counts. All of them keep the practice alive during a season when the bigger work is not possible.

A painter in maintenance mode is still a painter. The practice has not stopped. It has shrunk, on purpose, to fit the available life. When the season turns, the painter is still at the easel, still in the habit, still ready to scale back up. The painter who went to zero during the hard season has to rebuild everything when the season ends, and rebuilding is harder than maintaining.

"Maintenance mode is still motion. The habit is the thing. The work is what the habit produces."

Exercise: If this week is a hard one, pick three maintenance activities you can do in under fifteen minutes each. Clean brushes. Prime a panel. Look at a subject you want to paint later. Do a value study, or an even color study. Do one today. That is enough. You are still a painter.

---

2. The Phone in Another Room

If you only change one thing after reading this chapter, change this. The phone is the single most destructive force in a modern painting practice, and putting it in another room is the single most effective intervention.

Not face down on the taboret. Not on silent in your pocket. Not in airplane mode across the studio. In another room. Behind a closed door.

Ideally with the volume up so you can still hear it ring for emergencies, but physically separated from you while you work.

The reason this matters is not willpower. The reason is that the phone is designed by people much smarter than you to hijack your attention, and it succeeds even when you are trying to ignore it. The presence of the phone in your workspace costs you attention even when you are not looking at it. Every study that has been done on this says the same thing: the only reliable solution is physical distance.

I have tested this myself more times than I want to admit. The sessions where the phone is in another room are qualitatively different from the sessions where it is in the studio. Not a little different. A lot different. The mind has room to wander into the painting when it is not being pulled, every few minutes, by the gravity of a device in the corner of its awareness.

Try it once. Leave the phone in the kitchen for a two-hour session. Notice what happens. You may find, as I did, that the session feels longer and more productive than any phone-adjacent session you have had in months.

Idea: Get a basic kitchen timer. One of the old analog ones with a dial. Use it to time your studio sessions. You no longer need the phone in the studio for anything, including timing. The phone has lost its last legitimate reason to be there.

---

3. Thirty Minutes Is Enough

The belief that you need a full day to paint is the most destructive time-myth in artistic life. It keeps more painters out of the studio than any other single idea. And it is not true. It has never been true. Some of the best paintings in the world were made in sessions shorter than you think.

Thirty minutes is enough to do a color study. Thirty minutes is enough to work on one section of a larger painting. Thirty minutes is enough to solve a value problem in a thumbnail. Thirty minutes is enough to warm up the hand and eye, which is usually worth more than the finished product anyway.

The trick is to stop asking, "Do I have a full day?" and start asking, "Do I have thirty minutes?" You almost always have thirty minutes. They are hiding in places you are not currently using: the window between the alarm and the first meeting, the lunch hour when you would otherwise scroll, the half hour after dinner when the family disperses, the twenty minutes you would spend lingering on the couch at night.

Stop hoarding. Stop waiting. Thirty minutes of actual painting beats three hours of thinking about painting. Every time. Without fail.

**"You do not need a full day.
You need a closed door and a short clock."**

---

4. The Transition Ritual

One of the reasons life bleeds into the studio is that most artists do not have a real transition between the two. They walk out of a full kitchen, past a crying child, through an email on their phone, and directly into the studio, expecting to paint. The mind is still carrying everything from the walk. The painting gets what is left over, which is usually not much.

A transition ritual gives the mind a chance to leave one thing and arrive at another. It does not have to be elaborate. It can be sixty seconds. The point is that there is a deliberate threshold between life and studio, and crossing it signals to your body that the mode has changed.

Here are a few that painters I know have used. Pick one, try it for a week, see if the sessions feel different.

- **The hand-wash.** Before you pick up a brush, wash your hands slowly, thinking about nothing. The physical act of warm water and soap is a mental bridge.

- **The deep breath.** Three slow breaths before you touch anything. In through the nose, out through the mouth. Twenty seconds total.

- **The reference look.** Pick up your reference and look at it for one full minute without touching anything else. Just look. Let the subject enter your mind.

- **The brush in the water.** Dip one brush in clean water or medium and hold it for a moment before the first stroke.

- **The prayer.** For some, a short prayer of gratitude or asking for clarity. Seconds, not minutes. A quiet invitation to begin with an open hand.

What the ritual is does not matter. That the ritual exists does. It is the door between life and studio, and crossing it on purpose changes what happens on the other side.

---

5. Protected Time, Honored First

If you share your life with other people, your studio time will be negotiated whether you admit it or not. The only question is whether the negotiation is explicit or silent. Silent negotiations always go the same way: the studio loses.

Explicit negotiation means saying out loud, to the people you live with, what time you need and when. Not asking for permission. Telling them the plan and inviting them to help protect it. This is uncomfortable for many of us because we were raised to treat our own work as secondary, as indulgent, as something we should feel grateful to be allowed to do at all. That framing does not serve anyone, including the people we love. They do not want a martyr. They want the person who is alive and well and doing the thing they were made to do.

A few practical ways to protect the time.

- Name specific windows. "Tuesday and Thursday mornings from nine to eleven." Not "whenever I can."

- Put them on a shared calendar that everyone can see.

- Treat them with the same seriousness you would treat a job interview or a doctor's appointment. You would not skip those for laundry.

- When someone asks you to do something during that window, say: "I have a studio session then. How about two o'clock?" Do not apologize.

- If you cancel on yourself three times in a row, notice. That is a signal that the window is not working and needs to be re-negotiated, not that you need to try harder.

Bobbie and I have been married more than forty years. Most of what I know about protecting studio time, I know because I got it wrong for the first ten or fifteen of them. Early in our marriage I had a habit of disappearing into whatever I was working on without telling her when I would be out. I thought I was being unobtrusive. I was being thoughtless. The studio was getting the alive part of me, and the kitchen was getting the leftover part, and I did not see the trade I was making.

The thing that changed it was not a big fight. It was a conversation, probably in the kitchen, probably over coffee, where Bobbie said something simple about wanting to know when to expect me back. That was it. But when I heard her say it out loud, I understood. It was not that she wanted less of my painting. She wanted the painting and the person back at an appointed time, so that the person she had married was still findable at the end of the day.

We built a practice out of that conversation. I started telling her when I would be in the studio and when I would be out. She started treating those windows as real, which meant I had to start treating them as real too. The painting got better because the windows were protected. The marriage got better because the person came back when he said he would.

The painter who paints is lighter company than the painter who is silently resentful about not getting to paint. That is true. What is also true is that the painter who paints on a schedule his family can plan around is the best company of all. Everyone benefits. Especially the person you love most.

> *"The painter who paints is lighter company than the painter who is silently resentful about not getting to paint."*

---

6. The Studio Bookmark

Here is a trick that saves me more sessions than almost any other. At the end of every session, no matter how short or long, leave the studio in a state where tomorrow's session can begin in under three minutes. I call it a studio bookmark. It is a small act of love for your tomorrow-self.

Specifically: the next reference is already set up. The next panel or surface is already prepared. The colors you plan to use are noted on a piece of paper next to the palette. The first sentence of intent is written down. The thumbnail, if you did one, is taped to the edge of the easel.

When you walk in tomorrow, you do not have to figure anything out. You walk in, see the bookmark, and pick up where you left off. Three minutes to full paint-mode. No decision fatigue. No re-onboarding. No hunting for where you were.

The reason this matters so much for life-interrupted painters is that our studio time is rarely a long continuous block. It is a series of short sessions separated by days or weeks of life. Without a bookmark, each session has to begin from scratch, and beginning from scratch eats half the available time. With a bookmark, the short sessions stack together into something that feels continuous, because each one remembers the last.

Exercise: At the end of your next studio session, take two extra minutes to set a bookmark for tomorrow. Reference in place. Next thumbnail visible. One-sentence intent written on a scrap. See if your next session starts faster than usual.

---

7. Season Awareness

Not every season of life is a production season. Some seasons are for caregiving, for recovery, for transition, for grief, for the quiet work of becoming a different person than you were. Trying to produce at full speed during these seasons is not heroic. It is a failure to read the weather.

The practice of season awareness is simple: notice what season you are in, and adjust the expectations accordingly. A painter in a hard caregiving season does not need to be producing ten finished paintings a month. A painter recovering from illness does not need to match the output they had before. A painter in the first year after a loss does not need to be making their strongest work. Expectations calibrated for one season applied to a different one will grind you down fast.

Here are some of the seasons I have watched painters move through.

- **Early parenting.** Small windows. Fragmented sleep. The studio often has to wait for nap time or after bedtime. Maintenance mode is the default. Production is a gift, not an expectation.

- **Caregiving.** For a parent, a spouse, a child with ongoing needs. Energy is the scarcest resource. The practice shrinks to whatever fits inside the remaining capacity, and that is enough.

- **Illness and recovery.** Your own or someone you love. The body is busy healing. Painting may be therapeutic or it may be too much. Both are valid. Listen to the body.

- **Grief.** The first months after a loss. Work may be the last thing you want. It may also be the only thing that helps. There is no right answer. There is only the next hour.

- **Moves and transitions.** New house, new job, new city, new chapter. The studio is usually in boxes. Maintenance mode is unpacking one tool and making one mark. That counts.

- **Full production.** The rare season when everything is aligned and the work pours out. Enjoy it. Do not waste it wishing the other seasons were gone. They are part of the same life.

Season awareness is not an excuse to produce less forever. It is a way of honoring what is happening in your life and matching your expectations to it. The painter who recognizes a caregiving season and shifts into maintenance mode comes out of that season still a painter. The one who tries to produce at full speed through it often comes out of it too bitter or too burned out to come back at all.

---

8. The Body Comes First

You cannot paint well from an exhausted body. You cannot paint well from a dehydrated body. You cannot paint well from a body that has not slept. This is not a character flaw. It is physics. The eye, the hand, and the brain are all parts of a single system, and that system runs on sleep, water, food, and movement.

The painters I know who keep painting through decades of life are not the ones with the strongest willpower. They are the ones who take care of the vessel. They sleep seven or eight hours a night most nights. They drink water throughout the day. They eat real food at regular intervals. They walk, stretch, or move their bodies on a schedule. None of this is glamorous. All of it is what makes the work sustainable.

When the studio feels wrong and you cannot figure out why, check the body first. It is almost always at least part of the answer. A bad painting day that follows a bad night of sleep is not a painting problem. It is a sleep problem wearing a painting costume.

Here are the basics. Not a wellness program. Just the minimum for a painter to stay functional.

- Seven to eight hours of sleep most nights. Protect this like you protect studio time.

- Water within reach of the easel. Drink it regularly.

- Food before long sessions. A hungry painter is a distracted painter.

- Movement every day. A twenty-minute walk. A stretch routine. Anything that keeps the body from stiffening into the shape of the easel.

- Breaks during long sessions. Stand up. Look out a window. Drink water. Return.

   "The body is the ground the painting stands on. Neglect the ground and the painting falls."

9. Digital Hygiene Beyond the Phone

The phone is the biggest problem but it is not the only one. Modern life is full of digital drains that each seem harmless and together are devastating. Email open in a tab while you paint. Notifications on your laptop. The habit of checking something, anything, every few minutes. Podcasts that feel relaxing but keep the mind in word-mode instead of image-mode.

The goal is not to eliminate digital life. That is neither possible nor desirable. The goal is to protect the studio from it. Whatever you need to do to make the studio a low-input zone, do it.

A few practices that work.

- **The silent session.** No music, no podcast, no audiobook. Just the sound of the studio. Try it once. Notice what your mind starts hearing when the noise stops.

- **The single window.** If you must have your laptop open for reference, close every other tab. Just the reference. Nothing else.

- **Notifications off.** Every notification you can turn off on every device, turn off. Forever if possible. For the session at minimum.

- **The long walk.** Once a week, take a walk of at least thirty minutes with no phone and no podcast. It is about letting the mind settle into its natural shape again.

- **The morning grace period.** The first hour of the day, no screens. Coffee, light, quiet, maybe a reference, maybe a sketch. The mind you build in that hour is the mind you bring into the studio.

These are not ascetic rules. They are interventions against an environment that has been engineered to fragment attention. Painting requires whole attention. The modern world does not offer it for free. You have to protect it on purpose.

---

10. The Minimum Viable Session

The last idea in this chapter may be the most practical. Define, for yourself, what counts as a real session on the worst possible day. Not your best day. Your worst day. The day when you are tired and distracted and discouraged and have twenty minutes at most.

My minimum viable session is this. Phone in the kitchen. Studio door closed. Fifteen minutes of actual paint on actual surface. Could be a color note. Could be a value study. Could be twenty minutes of working on a larger piece. Does not have to be good. Has to happen.

That is my floor. The thing I can do no matter what the week has been.

Most weeks I do more. Some weeks I only do the minimum, and on those weeks I still get to say I painted. The streak continues. The habit holds. I am still a painter.

Your minimum should probably look different from mine. Yours should be calibrated to your actual worst day, not your ideal day. Make it little enough that you can do it even when you really do not want to. Make it specific enough that you know exactly what counts. Make it real enough that doing it feels like something, not like a consolation prize.

Once you have your minimum, use it on the days that would otherwise go to zero. Those are the days the minimum was made for. The minimum on a hard day protects the habit. The habit is what produces the work on the good days. Without the habit, the good days arrive and find nobody home.

**"The minimum on a hard day is not a consolation prize.
It is the reason the good days still find you at the easel."**

---

11. The Legacy Question

There is one more thing every working painter eventually has to face, and most of us put it off longer than we should.

What happens to the work when you are gone.

I do not mean this darkly. I mean it practically. A working painter over a long career accumulates paintings, studies, frames, panels, tools, records, files, client lists, unfinished pieces, and a thousand decisions embedded in the studio that only the painter fully understands. When the painter steps away, through retirement, through downsizing, through moving, or eventually through death. All of that becomes someone else's problem, unless the painter has done the work of making it legible.

Most painters do not do this work. They assume there will be time later. Later often arrives in ways nobody planned for, and the people who inherit the studio are left trying to reconstruct a life's work from boxes, with no map, and usually under emotional pressure. The kindest thing you can do for the people who love you is not to leave them with that puzzle.

The good news is that someone has finally written the book that walks a working artist through exactly how to do this, and I am going to point you to it.

My friend and colleague, Mary Longe, author and advisor specializing in helping artists and their families navigate the art marketplace, has written a guide called The Art Legacy Compass. It is the most practical, thoughtful, field-tested resource I know of for helping an artist organize a studio, document a career, plan for the eventual handoff of the work, and support the heirs and executors who will one day step into the studio without you. It covers the inventory work, the income streams, the provenance records, the digital accounts, the downsizing decisions, and the specific instructions an artist can leave behind so the people left in charge are not guessing. It is written for living artists who want to get ahead of the question, and it is equally useful for executors and family members who have been handed the task without preparation.

I cannot recommend it more highly. Every working painter should have a copy. Not to read once and shelve, but to work through a few pages at a time, in short sessions, until the studio is organized and the future is no longer a puzzle waiting to ambush the people you love.

You will find Mary's book and her other resources through her website. Look up the Art Legacy Compass. Start with Step One. Work in short focused sessions the same way I have asked you to work in every other chapter of this book. A weekend of legacy work now will save your family weeks of confusion later, and it will free you to paint the next painting without the background weight of an unfinished plan. www.marylonge. com

That is Chapter 5's final permission. Protect the habit. Protect the body. Protect the windows. And protect the people who will one day have to step into your studio and figure out what to do without you.

Questions to Sit With

Take these slowly. The life chapter is the one most of us have the hardest time being honest about, because the answers tend to implicate people we love.

- What season am I in right now? Production? Maintenance? Something harder?

- When was the last time I painted for thirty minutes? What would it take to paint for thirty minutes tomorrow?

- Where is my phone while I paint? If it is in the studio, what am I afraid I will miss?

- Do I have protected studio time that the people I live with know about? Is it working?

- What is my minimum viable session? Have I ever written it down?

- Am I currently pushing through when I should be resting, or resting when I should be pushing through? How can I tell?

- What transition ritual, if any, do I currently have between life and studio? What could I add?

- What would it look like to leave a bookmark at the end of my next session?

A Closing Thought

The life you have is the only life in which you get to paint. There is no other one waiting in the wings for when things calm down. The settled, spacious, uninterrupted season you keep expecting is a story we tell ourselves to explain why we are not painting today. It will never arrive, because it does not exist.

What exists is this week, with its interruptions and its obligations and its fatigue. And this week is enough. Not because it is ideal. Because it is the only week you really have. The painter who waits for the ideal week never paints. The painter who works inside the real week, in thirty-minute increments, on tired days, around the edges of other responsibilities, is the one who ends up with a body of work.

Protect the habit when the output has to shrink. Shrink honestly and without shame. A maintenance session is a real session. A little painting is a real painting. Fifteen minutes is a real fifteen minutes. Nothing about any of this is a consolation prize.

The life you have is the life your paintings will come out of. All of it. The tired days and the discouraged days and the full weeks and the hard seasons. Paint from inside that life, not around it. The painter who learns this never has to wait for the perfect conditions again, because they finally understand that the perfect conditions are the ones they are standing in right now.

Of the seven ways of adding value, this chapter was mostly about **Less** and **More.** Less of what is eating your attention: the phone, the open tabs, the endless yes, the guilt about protecting an hour for your own work. More of what feeds the practice: maintenance mode when the tank is low, protected windows when the tank is full, a bookmark for tomorrow, a minimum viable session on the days that would otherwise go to zero. Less and More are a pair of scissors. One blade without the other just waves in the air. Together, they cut a life into a shape a painter can live inside.

"The life you have is the only life in which you get to paint."

CHAPTER SIX

The Source

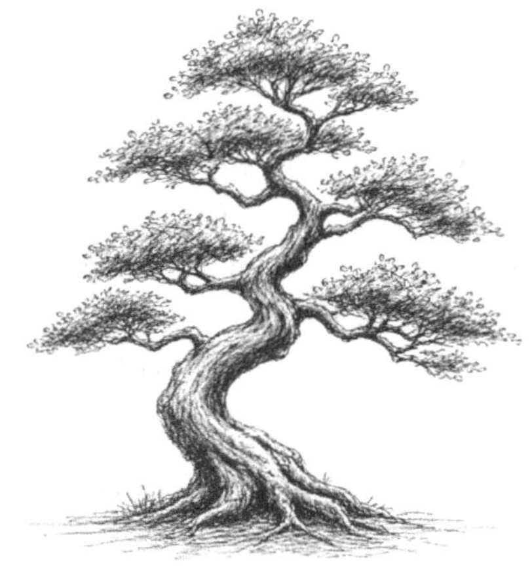

Wonder, Attention, and the Why Beneath the How

You can paint a competent painting without any of this chapter. The brush still moves. The values still work. The color still sings. From the outside, nothing looks wrong.

But you know something is. You know it the way a musician knows when the technique is perfect and the music is dead. You know it the way a preacher knows when the sermon was clever and nobody was moved. You know it because you used to feel something at the easel that you do not feel anymore, and no amount of good craft is making up for whatever it is you have lost.

This is the chapter that is hardest to write and the easiest to get wrong. It is about the thing beneath the thing. The source the work is supposed to come from. The why that sits underneath every how. If Design gives clarity and Story gives meaning and Freshness gives life, this chapter is about where Design, Story, and Freshness come from in the first place.

I do not want to turn this into a sermon. I am not qualified to preach, and you did not pick up a book about studio practice to be preached at. What I will try to do is name, as plainly as I can, something almost every long-working painter eventually discovers: that the outer problems of the studio all have an inner counterpart, and that when the inner side dries up, the outer side starts failing in ways the outer tools cannot fix.

"Wonder precedes work.
If you have lost the wonder, you will not fix it at the easel."

Some of you who are reading this share my faith. Some of you do not. Some of you are figuring it out. I have tried to write a chapter that serves all of you, because the underlying questions are the same regardless of where you stand. Why am I doing this? What is the work for? When did I stop feeling the wonder, and how do I find my way back? Those questions belong to every painter who has ever picked up a brush and meant it.

I spent a Saturday painting at Lincoln Park Conservatory in Chicago a few years ago. The painting itself is not the point. The people walking past me were the point, and one of them in particular.

Most of them moved the way most people move. Some paused to say "nice picture." Children looked at the painting first and then at my eyes to figure out whose painting it was. Older people did the opposite. They looked at my eyes first, and sometimes not at the painting at all.

One of them, an older gentleman named Lou, stopped walking entirely. He had pale blue eyes, the kind of blue that has been looking at the world for a long time. He held my gaze for what must have been two full minutes, which is longer than most strangers will hold anything. We talked about age, and about life, and a little bit about what he called "the old country." I do not remember the specifics of what he said. I remember his eyes, and I remember the feeling of being looked at by someone who was there.

I finished that painting, but what I remember from that day is Lou, not the painting. For a long time afterward, I felt slightly embarrassed about that. A proper professional, I told myself, would have been focused on the work. It took me a while to understand that the work and the encounter were the same thing. Sometimes I think I am really a connector of people cleverly disguised as a plein air painter, and that the painting is the excuse that gives me permission to stand in a public place long enough for Lou to find me.

This is part of what "sit and look" has come to mean for me. It is not only about looking at trees and puddles and doorways. It is also about letting people find you when you have put yourself somewhere long enough to be found.

What Goes Wrong

The source dries up slowly. It is almost never a single event. It is a quiet drift that you do not notice until one day you realize the water that used to rise when you stood at the easel is not rising anymore, and has not been rising for a while, and you are not sure when it stopped.

Here is what the drift looks like from the inside.

You still paint. You still finish things. The paintings still sell, or they still go into the show, or they still get posted. From the outside, everything is working. On the inside, something has shifted. You used to paint because you saw something and had to say something back to it. Now you paint because you have a deadline, or a gallery expects another piece, or it is what you do and you do not know who you are if you stop. The work has become output. The easel has become a job site. The subject has become a thing to render. Somewhere along the way, the reason for making the painting got replaced by the obligation to make the painting, and the replacement happened so gradually that you did not notice.

Or it looks like this. You scroll past another artist's work on your phone and feel something you used to only feel at the easel, and the feeling is immediately followed by envy, measurement, anxiety about your own place in the hierarchy. The scrolling ends. The feelings stay. You get to the studio an hour later and the painting in front of you feels pointless, and you cannot remember why you cared about it this morning.

Or like this. You finish a painting you know is good. You look at it. You wait for the feeling that used to follow finishing a good painting. The feeling does not come. You photograph the painting, post it, answer the comments. The comments are kind. You feel nothing. That night, lying in bed, you wonder if you have finally become the kind of painter who cannot feel anything at all, and if that is what it takes to keep producing at the level you have been producing.

Every one of these is a signal that the source has gone quiet. Not that it is gone. That it has gone quiet, and nobody has been listening.

The Beliefs That Keep the Source Dry

"My value is in what I produce."

This is the deepest and most destructive of the beliefs, because it fuses identity to output. When you make something good, you feel good. When you do not make something, or what you make is weak, you feel worthless. Your worth bobs up and down on a chart of your productivity. No soul can stand this for long. It turns painting into a constant self-audit, and a constant self-audit is the opposite of the open, curious, attentive mind that makes good work.

"If this doesn't lead to something measurable, it doesn't count."

This is the market mind. It treats every painting as an investment that must return. If a study does not become a finished painting, the study was a waste. If a finished painting does not sell, the painting was a failure. If a workshop does not directly pay for itself, the workshop was indulgence. The market mind is a useful servant and a terrible master. When it takes over, art becomes transactions, and transactions have a way of slowly killing the thing they were supposed to measure.

"I used to love this. I don't know what happened."

This one hurts because it is usually true, and because the answer is not a mystery. What happened is that the loving got squeezed out by the performing. The love was not destroyed. It was displaced. It is waiting, underneath the performing, for someone to come back and notice it again. This chapter is mostly about how to come back.

"I have to earn the right to make art."

No. You already have the right. You were given it the first time you picked up a crayon as a child and made a mark and felt something. The permission is not transactional. It is not based on whether you are good enough or successful enough or productive enough. It is a birthright, and nobody can revoke it, and you do not have to audition for it every morning before you walk into the studio.

The Smorgasbord: Ten Ways to Return to the Source

What follows is a collection of practices, not a checklist you have to finish. None of them will fix the source problem in a single day. All of them, done consistently and gently, will slowly restore the thing that has gone quiet. The water will rise again. It always does, if you make room for it.

These practices are not mystical. They are practical. They are repeatable acts of attention that remind the mind and body where wonder lives and how to find it again. You do not need to believe anything in particular to do them. You need to be willing to stop, look, and wait for something that cannot be forced.

---

1. Sit and Look

This is the simplest practice in the book and the one most likely to be dismissed as too simple to matter. Sit down somewhere outside. Look at something. A tree. A puddle. A branch. A fence line. Do not plan a painting. Do not take a photograph. Do not think about composition. Just look for ten minutes.

That is the practice.

The reason it works is that most of us have forgotten how to look without acquiring. We see a subject and immediately begin processing it: would this make a painting, where is the focal point, what is the value structure, is the light good enough. The processing is useful at the easel. It is destructive everywhere else. It turns every encounter with the world into a transaction, and after enough transactions, the world stops offering itself to us as anything more than raw material.

Ten minutes of looking without acquiring restores the older way of seeing. The way you looked at things before you were a painter. The way a
child looks, or the way a person looks at something they love. This is the
seeing the painting is supposed to come from. Without it, the painting
has nothing to stand on.

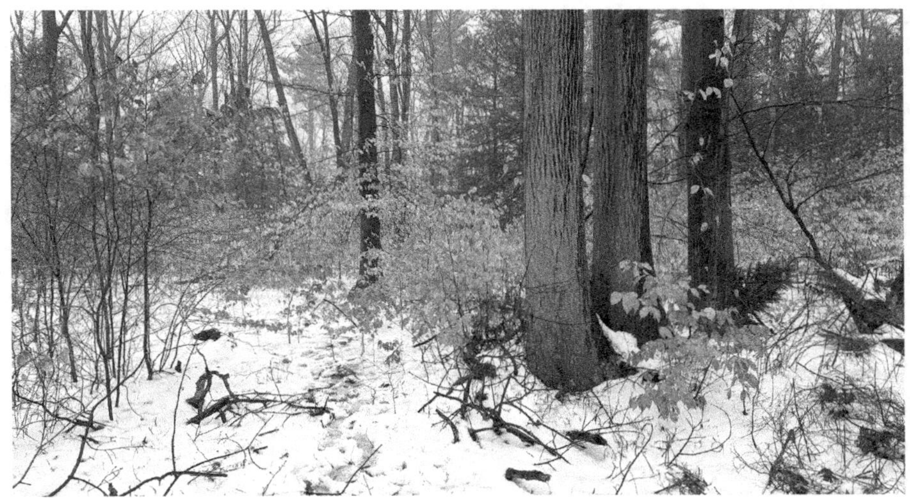

Marigold Woods, Holland, Michigan

While you are looking, ask yourself one question: what is alive here?
Not what is pretty. Not what is impressive. Not what would make a good
painting. What has tension, contrast, a question you cannot quite answer? What has some kind of pulse in it? The answer is usually not what
you expected when you sat down. The pulse is in the dented mailbox,
not the picture-perfect flower bed. The pulse is in the way the light hits
a doorway at four in the afternoon, not the sweeping vista. Go for the
overlooked things. The things the camera would miss because it does
not know how to care.

The Irish poet and philosopher John O'Donohue had a line I come
back to often. He wrote in Walking in Wonder that the imagination can
always go deeper than what the mind first sees. The mind names things.
The imagination finds meaning. The mind looks at a tree and thinks
tree. The imagination looks at the same tree and begins to find the story

inside it. The sitting-and-looking practice is how you get the mind out of the way long enough for the imagination to do its quieter, deeper work.

Some days nothing will happen during the ten minutes. You will sit and look and feel restless and wonder if you are doing it right. That is part of it. Do it anyway. The days when nothing seems to happen are building something underneath that will show up later, in a painting you will make six months from now that surprises you.

Exercise: Tomorrow morning, before you do anything else, sit somewhere outside for ten minutes. Look at one thing. No phone, no sketchbook, no plan. Ask the question: what is alive here? Notice what, if anything, shifts by minute eight.

---

2. The Walk Without a Camera

Go for a walk. A real one. Forty-five minutes or an hour, somewhere outdoors if possible. Leave your phone at home, or leave it in your pocket in airplane mode. Do not take pictures. Do not plan paintings. Do not listen to anything. Walk and look and breathe.

This sounds so simple it cannot possibly matter. It matters more than almost anything else in this chapter. Most modern painters have lost the ability to be alone with their eyes for an hour. We have been trained by our devices to document everything, to convert every experience into content, to store rather than absorb. The walk without a camera is a protest against that training. It is a return to the older practice of taking a landscape in without needing to take it with you.

John Muir walked through the Sierra Nevada for months at a time with almost nothing in his pockets and a small notebook that he rarely used. He was not collecting material for later. He was letting the mountains work on him. The journals he did keep were not records of the country. They were records of what the country had done to him. That is a different thing, and it is the thing the walk without a camera teaches you.

You will be surprised, after a walk like this, how much you remember. The memory is different from a photograph. It is fuller, slower, and more yours. The colors are slightly wrong but somehow more true. The shapes have a weight that photographs never catch. This is the kind of memory a painting can come from. Photographs give you data. Walks give you something the data cannot reach.

"Going to the mountains is going home." John Muir

---

3. The Gratitude Practice

This is more specific than the usual gratitude advice, because it is aimed at a particular person: the artist. Spend sixty seconds, at the start of a studio session, being specifically grateful for something about the craft itself.

Not gratitude for your life in general. Gratitude for this: the tubes of color on your palette, which are a technological miracle that would have stunned any painter before the nineteenth century. The brushes in your hand, which are made from animal hair by people who have spent generations perfecting them. The panel or paper in front of you, which exists because somebody grew a tree or pressed a fiber. The light in the room. The eye that still works. The hand that still obeys. The time that has been given to you for this.

Sixty seconds. Not a prayer necessarily, though for some of us it is one. Just a deliberate noticing of the goodness of the tools and the moment. A refusal to take any of it for granted.

The practice works because gratitude is incompatible with the market mind. You cannot be in a performance anxiety spiral and also be noticing how remarkable it is that you get to do this at all. The two states cannot occupy the same mind at the same time. Gratitude, even for sixty seconds, resets the mood the session was about to begin in.

I learned this one the hard way, after too many sessions that began in a tight-shouldered hurry and ended in frustration. Now I start most sessions with a minute of noticing that nothing about this morning was guaranteed. It changes the paintings. I cannot prove it in any scientific way. I know it in the way a painter knows things.

"Gratitude is incompatible with the market mind. The two cannot occupy the same mind at the same time."

"Gratitude is incompatible with the market mind. The two cannot occupy the same mind at the same time."

---

4. Return to the Small Wonder

Big wonder is rare. A sunset over the Grand Canyon. A storm over the Pacific. The Milky Way over a dark-sky park. We wait for these and get almost none of them. If we only feel wonder in the presence of bigness, we will feel wonder about six times in our lives.

Small wonder is everywhere and we are usually too busy to notice it. The way dew gathers on a spiderweb. The color of a brick wall in late afternoon. The shape of a cloud. The pattern of rain on a puddle. The curve of a shadow under a leaf. Any of these, looked at properly, is more than enough to make a whole painting and a whole life.

The practice is simple: set a small intention to find one small wonder a day, and do not let the day end until you have found it. Not a grand wonder. Something you walked past without seeing last Tuesday. Something you would have missed if you had not been looking.

Most painters wait for inspiration to show up. Better painters bring curiosity and see what happens. Inspiration is unreliable. Curiosity is a muscle you can train.

John O'Donohue, writing in Walking in Wonder, put this difference into words better than I can. He said:

> *"The lovely thing about the imagination is that, whereas the mind often sees change and thinks everything is lost, the imagination can always go deeper than the actual experience of the loss and find something else in it. There is an amazing difference between the way the mind sees something and the way the imagination sees something."*

That line changed how I walk through the world. The mind looks at a scene and takes inventory. The imagination looks at the same scene and asks what is underneath. The mind is useful. The imagination is essential. And the imagination only shows up when you have given it room to, which usually means slowing down long enough to let the wonder reach you.

I have built a whole practice around this, which I call Wonder Walking™. The core is simple. Before you paint, you walk. You look. You pause. You let a scene work on you instead of you working on it. You start with gratitude for the chance to look closely, and then you ask the question that cuts through almost everything else: what is alive here? The answer is rarely what the mind would have chosen. It is usually smaller, stranger, and truer. Mix imagination with a dose of attention, and something numb becomes something worth painting.

When you start doing this, you will notice two things. First, that the wonders are genuinely everywhere, and you have been walking past them for years. Second, that you start seeing them in the subjects you were already planning to paint, and your paintings start getting better without you quite understanding why. The better is coming from the looking. The looking is coming from the practice. The practice is coming from a decision you made to stop expecting the wonder to announce itself.

You can download the free Wonder Walking booklet here:
www.fairviewfinder.com/store/p/wonder-walking

"The mind names things. The imagination finds meaning."

Exercise: Today, find one small wonder that you would normally walk past. Ask what is alive about it. Look at it for thirty seconds. Do not photograph it. Carry it with you for the rest of the day.

5. Read Something That Stirs You

The inner life needs feeding. The same way the body needs food and water, the soul of an artist needs to take in things that remind it why it bothers. Not instructional books about painting technique. Those are useful but they feed a different part of you. I mean things that stir, things that awaken, things that remind you the world is stranger and larger and more beautiful than you had been treating it.

For me these writers are specific. Annie Dillard on the pilgrim's eye. C.S. Lewis on the stab of joy. John Muir, because he walked into wilderness and came out transfigured. John O'Donohue, whose Walking in Wonder shows how imagination can always go deeper than what the mind first sees. Your writers will be different, and they should be. What matters is that they exist, and that you read them slowly, not for information, but for the slow work they do on the part of you that painting also comes from. Ten minutes a day of something that stirs you will do more for your work than an hour a day of how-to content, because the how-to content teaches the hand and the stirring teaches the heart, and the heart is what the hand is supposed to be following.

6. The Silent Studio

Try painting without any background sound. No music. No podcast. No audiobook. Just the sound of the brush on the panel and the small rustlings of the room. Try it for a single session and see what happens.

Most of us fill the studio with sound as a matter of habit. We tell ourselves it helps us focus, or that the right music puts us in the right mood, or that we need company during the long hours. Some of this is true some of the time. A lot of it is a reflex against a silence we have learned to fear.

The silent studio is an experiment in listening to what is there. What you hear, at first, is a lot of internal noise. Your own worried thoughts, your lists, your comparisons. Under that, eventually, you hear something quieter: the painting itself, and your own attention, and the thing underneath both that has been waiting to speak.

You do not have to paint in silence forever. I do not. Some sessions are for music and some are for podcasts and a few are for silence. The point is to learn that the silent option exists, and to use it when the soul needs a little more room to breathe than the music was giving it. A few silent sessions a month will teach you something about your own work that no soundtrack ever could.

Exercise: Your next session, paint in complete silence for the first thirty minutes. No music, no podcast, no phone. See what you notice. See what you hear.

---

7. The Witness, Not the Product

This is a reframe, not a practice. It is a change in how you think about what a painting actually is, and for many artists it changes everything downstream.

The market frame says a painting is a product. It is made to be sold, or shown, or displayed, or evaluated. Its purpose is external. Its success is measured by what happens to it after it leaves your studio. This frame is not wrong, exactly. Paintings do leave the studio and do have lives in the world. But when the market frame becomes the only frame, it starts to corrode the making, because it shifts the attention from the subject to the audience.

The witness frame says something different. A painting is not a product. A painting is a record of what you saw and how you saw it. It is your testimony about a particular moment, a particular light, a particular way the world arrived in your eye on a particular morning. It exists to say: this was here, I was here, and this is what the meeting looked like. The painting is the meeting, not the thing produced by the meeting.

When you hold the witness frame, a lot of the pressure around the painting changes. You are not auditioning for the market. You are reporting what you saw. A bad report is still a report. A painting that nobody buys still did its work, because the work was the witnessing, and the witnessing already happened. The painting is just the evidence.

This reframe is not magic. It will not make you stop caring about whether paintings sell. But it will put the selling in its proper place: after the witnessing, not before. The witnessing is what you are responsible for. The selling is weather. You plant the garden. You do not control the rain.

***"A painting is not a product.
It is a record of what you saw and how you saw it.
The painting is the evidence of the meeting."***

---

8. Playing Without a Goal

When was the last time you made a painting with no purpose whatsoever? Not a study that was going to teach you something. Not a gift for someone. Not a warm-up for a real painting. Not a piece for a show. Just a painting made for no reason except that you felt like moving some paint around.

For most working artists, the answer is: not recently. The studio has become too serious a place for play. Everything has to justify itself. Every session has to produce something. Every brushstroke has to count. And the net result is that a painter who started painting because it was the most fun they had ever had has turned painting into another form of performance, and has forgotten what fun felt like.

The cure is to make a point of playing. Deliberately. Regularly. Without apology. Once a week, or once a month, or whenever the seriousness is starting to choke the life out of the work, set aside an hour and make something just because. Use weird colors. Use wrong subjects. Use materials you do not usually use. Break your own rules. See what happens.

You will discover a few things. You will discover that playful paintings are often the ones you like best, months later, when you come across them in a drawer. You will discover that your voice, which had gotten quieter under the weight of performance, comes back louder during play. You will discover that play is not the opposite of serious work. It is the ground serious work grows out of. The artists who play are almost always the ones who also make the most interesting serious work, because the play is where the discoveries happen, and the discoveries are what the serious work eventually reports on.

Idea: Designate one panel a week as a play panel. Nothing serious is allowed on it. Whatever you make on it is for nobody but you. Most of them will be nothing. A few of them will surprise you. All of them will loosen you up.

---

9. The Threshold Practice

Before you enter the studio, stop at the door. For five seconds. Breathe once. Let whatever you were carrying into the studio set itself down on the other side of the threshold. Cross it on purpose.

This is a small ceremony, and it takes almost no time, but it does something important. It turns the studio back into a particular kind of place. Not just another room. A place where a particular kind of attention happens. The threshold is the line between ordinary life and the place where wonder has permission to show up.

Artists used to understand thresholds intuitively. They kept their studios in separate buildings. They walked to them. They arrived. Now we mostly work in converted rooms in the same houses where we do everything else, and the threshold has disappeared, and with it one of the supports that used to hold the practice together.

You cannot always build a separate studio building. You can always build a threshold. A pause at the door. A specific breath. A word said to yourself, silently or aloud. Over time, this ritual tells your mind: we are entering the place now. Let the other things go. The other things can wait. This is what we are here for.

Some of us, including me, make the threshold a moment of prayer. Not elaborate. Just a short asking to see what is in front of me and to make something honest from it. Others make it a breath, a stretch, a hand on the door frame. The specific form is not important. The line is.

> *"Return to the doorway. That is where wonder lives. Not in the room, not at the easel. At the place where you step across."*

---

10. Remember Why You Started

Years ago, Bobbie and I were painting plein air with our dear friend Valerie near a church schoolyard in Schaumburg, Illinois. Spring after-

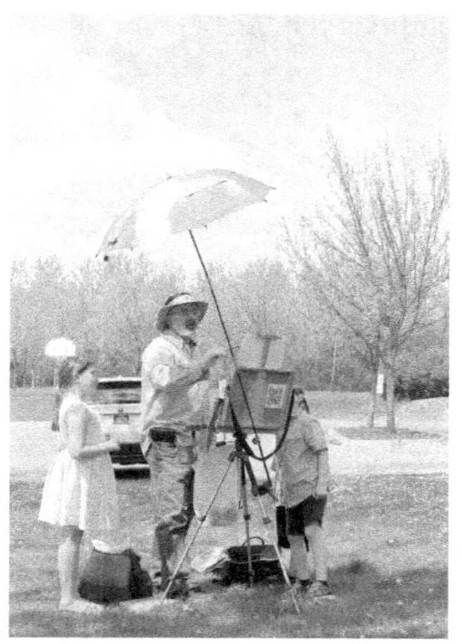

noon, warm light, ordinary day. I had my easel set up and was about an hour into an oil study when a bell rang inside the school and the doors burst open. Dozens of children came running out for recess, and within a minute, half of them had formed a loose ring around our three easels.

They asked the questions children always ask. What are you doing. Can I do that. How long did that take. Does the paint come off your hands. Why are you standing outside. I answered the first few without much trouble. Then one of them, I do not remember which one, asked the question that knocked me over.

"Why do you paint?"

I stood there with a wet brush in my hand and a child looking up at me with the kind of attention no adult ever gives you, and I could not answer the question. I said something like "to understand the light" or "to see better," and the child nodded politely and ran off to look at Bobbie's and Valerie's easels. But I stood there for the next several minutes not painting, because the question had opened something I had not known was closed.

I have been trying to answer that question properly ever since. Sometimes I think the entire practice of painting is just the long, slow, ongoing answer to a question asked by a seven-year-old on a playground in Schaumburg. When I am at my best in the studio, I am painting toward a better answer to that question. When I am at my worst, I have forgotten the question was ever asked.

If you have forgotten your own version of that question, go find it. It was asked of you once, probably by a child, or a younger version of yourself, or a teacher, or a grandparent. The answer is still there, waiting for you to come back and try again. The reason you started is closer to the truth of why you paint than any of the sophisticated reasons you have invented since then.

When the source has dried up, one of the most direct fixes is to deliberately remember the moment your own question got asked. Sit down with a cup of something hot. Close your eyes. Go back to the earliest moment you can remember wanting to make pictures. What did it feel like? What were you hoping to do? What were you seeing that you wanted to say back to? The memory will come slowly, and some of it will be invented, and that is fine. You are not writing a deposition. You are reconnecting with a self who knew something important and has been waiting for you to come find it again.

"The reason you started is closer to the truth of why you paint than any of the sophisticated reasons you have invented since then."

---

11. Finding Your Tap Root Words

Section 10 asked you to remember why you started. This section gives you a way to carry that remembering into every studio session, in three words.

I call it the Tap Root exercise. I use it in every workshop I teach, and it does something I have not found another exercise do quite the same way. It takes the abstract question of "why do you paint" and turns it into three specific words a painter can carry in their pocket and bring to the easel every morning.

How the exercise works

Sit somewhere still. Close your eyes. Take a few slow breaths and let your mind travel backward into your childhood. Do not force it. Let the memories come.

Think about the things you did as a child that made you come alive. Not the things you were praised for. Not the things you were told you were good at. The things that lit you up from the inside. The things you could disappear into. The things that made time fall away.

Now ask yourself one question. *Why?*

Maybe the first answer is, *because it was fun.* Good. Ask again. Why was it fun? Whatever answer comes, ask why again. Keep going. Five times is usually enough. Each answer takes you a little deeper, past the surface, closer to the tap root. Most of us stop too early. The first answer is rarely the truest one. The truest one is buried a few layers down, where the real current runs.

Once you reach that deeper answer, give it a name. One word if possible. A strong word. A clean word. A word that feels alive in your mouth.

Then do it again with another childhood memory. And again, with a third.

My three words

When I do this exercise, the three words I come back with are these.

Discovery. Adventure. Story.

Those are not slogans. They are roots. They are old, buried things that still feed the tree.

When I bring those three words into the studio before a session, I am not just setting an intention. I am calling something back to life. I am reaching down into childhood and pulling up the energy that first made me want to look, wander, imagine, and make. I am inviting that childlike spirit into the room again, only now it comes with decades of design, observation, experience, failure, and practice behind it.

That changes the session. I stop painting like someone trying to prove something and start painting like someone on the trail of something. The work becomes less about performance and more about pursuit.

Why this works

Psychology has a name for what this exercise does. Somatic therapists talk about glimmers, a term coined by Deb Dana. Glimmers are the opposite of triggers. Where triggers put the nervous system on alert, glimmers are small micro-moments of safety, beauty, or joy that return the body to ease and presence. The tap root words are your portable glimmers. Three words that reliably return you to the childlike state the work wants to come from.

In the Christian contemplative tradition, there is a similar idea called vocation, from the Latin vocare, to call. It means returning to the original calling beneath the current performance of it. That is what the tap root exercise does. It takes you back to the call before the career, the wonder before the technique, the child before the professional.

I am not claiming tap root words are therapy. They are not. They are a studio practice that draws from the same well. You do not need to believe any particular framework to do the exercise. You need to be willing to close your eyes, travel backward, ask why a few times, and listen for what comes up.

Your words will be different from mine, and they should be.

Everyone's childhood is different. What lit me up may not light you up. Your three words may be completely different from mine, and they should be. That is the point. One painter may come back with refuge, wonder, order. Another may find mischief, tenderness, risk. Another may uncover solitude, rhythm, beauty. None of these are wrong. They are roots, not slogans.

When the work grows stale, when your painting starts to feel overly trained or too careful to breathe, go back to the tap root. Ask what first made you feel alive. Ask why, and then why again. Follow the answers down until you hit something real. Name it. Bring it with you into the studio.

You may find that the child still knows something the adult has forgotten.

Exercise: This week, set aside thirty quiet minutes. Take yourself back to childhood. Find three specific memories of moments when time fell away. Ask why. Ask why five times for each memory. Write down the word you land on. At the end of thirty minutes, you should have three words. Write them on an index card. Tape it to the edge of your easel. Before your next painting session, read them out loud. Notice what changes.

"The child still knows something the adult has forgotten.
The tap root is the root that remembers."

Questions to Sit With

These are the slowest questions in the book. Do not try to answer them all in one sitting. Pick one. Sit with it for a week. Let the answer arrive, or not arrive. Both are useful.

- When was the last time I felt genuine wonder at something, inside or outside the studio?

- What am I currently painting for? And is that reason the one I want to be painting for?

- Who or what made me want to paint in the first place? How far am I from that original impulse?

- What does it look like, in my life, when the market mind is running the show? How do I recognize it?

- What would change if I treated my next painting as a witness, not a product?

- When was the last time I played in the studio, with no goal and no audience?

- What book, poet, or writer has stirred me recently? If the answer is none, when did I last let one?

- What would my threshold practice look like, if I built one tomorrow?

A Closing Thought

The source is not a well you can dig deeper into. It is a spring. It arrives from somewhere you did not make and cannot control, and your job is not to produce it but to receive it. The practices in this chapter are all variations on the same basic move: making room, slowing down, paying attention, refusing to let the market mind or the production mind or the comparison mind drown out the quieter voice that has been there the whole time.

Some days the voice is loud. Some days it is almost inaudible. Some seasons it feels like it has gone away completely. The seasons of absence are real, and they do not mean you have lost the gift. They mean you are in a quieter part of the long conversation, and the conversation will resume when both parties are ready. Your job in the quiet seasons is the same as your job in the loud ones: show up, pay attention, and be ready to notice if something starts speaking again. When you cannot hear anything at all, go back to your tap root words. The child who first came alive through making is still in there, and three words is usually enough to find them again.

Painting is not only labor. It is labor shaped by love, by attention, by wonder, by the willingness to keep looking at the world as though it might still surprise you. When those are present, the work is alive, and the work alive is worth all the rest of the effort. When they are absent, the work can still be competent, but you and the painting both know the difference.

The eleven practices in this chapter are not a system. They are invitations. Take the ones that speak to you. Leave the rest. Return to them next year. The source is patient. It has been there the whole time, and it is there now, and it will be there when you come back. Your only job is to build a life in which you can occasionally show up where it lives and be quiet long enough to hear it.

Then paint what you heard.

Of the seven ways of adding value, this chapter was mostly about **Fun** and **Different.** Fun, because the source is what makes painting feel alive instead of dutiful, and no painting made from duty alone will ever move a viewer the way a painting made from wonder does. Different, because wonder is the part of the work that cannot be copied, borrowed, or faked. It is the part that only you can bring, because it rises from what only you have seen. When the source is flowing, Fun and Different arrive together, and the viewer picks up on it without knowing why,

---

> **"Painting is attention shaped by love.**
> **Everything else is just craft."**

Special Cases

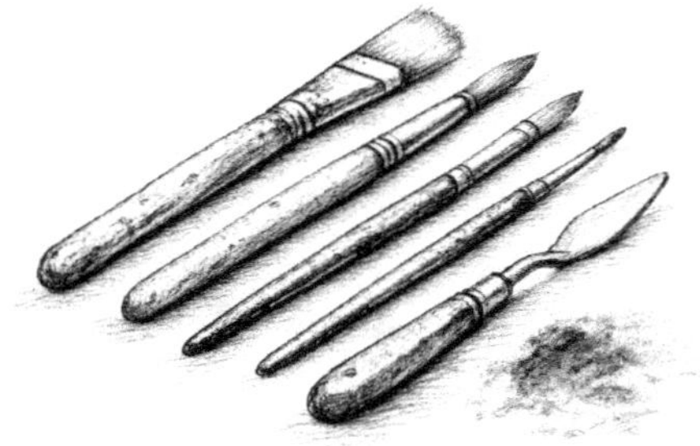

The Problems the Other Chapters Didn't Reach

The first six chapters cover most of what goes wrong in a studio. The room, the routine, the mind, the canvas, the life, the source. Those six account for ninety percent of the trouble a painter will run into over a working lifetime. If you fix those six, you will be a better painter than most.

But there are ten other problems that need their own attention. They are not fringe cases. They are common enough that nearly every working artist will meet several of them, and they are specific enough that the general advice in the other chapters does not quite reach them. A watercolorist's trouble is not the same as an oil painter's trouble. A plein air painter has problems a studio painter never encounters. A teaching artist has a particular kind of drought that only other teaching artists fully understand. A painter who has just had a successful year has a set of problems that would sound like bragging to anyone who has not had one.

This chapter is a collection of those special cases. Each section is short. Each one is self-contained. You do not have to read them in order. Skip the ones that do not apply to your situation. Return to the ones that do. Think of it as a small book of case studies, bound into the larger book, for when the other chapters did not quite answer your question.

**"Most painters will meet at least half of these problems.
Most of us pretend we are the only ones who have."**

If any of these feel like they were written specifically for you, that is not an accident. They were written for the many of us who have been exactly where you are, and who have mostly felt alone in it, because nobody talks about these particular troubles out loud.

1. Medium-Specific Resets

Not every medium fails the same way, and not every reset fits every medium. The oil painter scrapes. The watercolorist cannot scrape and has to deal with loss differently. The gouache painter lives somewhere between. The acrylic painter races the clock. Each medium has its own character, its own gifts, and its own traps. Knowing the traps of your medium is half the solution.

Oil

Oil is the most forgiving medium, and that is both its greatest gift and its greatest danger. You can scrape. You can wipe. You can repaint the same passage fifteen times. The paint stays open for hours or days. You can come back tomorrow and keep going. All of this is wonderful, and all of this is why oil painters overwork their paintings more than any other group.

The reset for an oil painter in trouble is almost always the same: scrape. Not a section. The whole painting, or at least the whole area that is giving you trouble. Take a palette knife and scrape it flat until you have a ghost of the image and a clean working surface. Then restate the big shapes in fresh paint. Most of the time, the painting comes back alive in the next twenty minutes, because the scrape forces you to simplify what you were overcomplicating.

The other reset for oil is the wipe. A clean rag with a little solvent, and you can erase back to a tone you can work from. This is less drastic than a scrape but often equally effective, especially in the early stages when the paint is still soft.

A Story from Cedarburg

Let me tell you how this works in the field. In 2024 I was painting at the Paint Cedarburg Plein Air Event, set up on the banks of Cedar Creek at Boy Scout Park. Across the river was the Anvil restaurant, with a cluster of red umbrellas that had caught my eye from the start. That was my painting. Or it was supposed to be.

An hour in, I had lost the plot. The painting was turning into a tight architectural illustration. Every window in its place. Every brick lovingly rendered. All facts and no life. I could feel it going wrong but I could not see my way out. I kept adding detail, which is what painters do when they are lost and afraid to stop.

Bobbie walked up behind me, took a look, and said, "It looks dead."

That was the whole critique. Three words. No sugar coating. After forty-plus years of marriage she has earned the right to speak plainly, and I love her for never wasting it on flattery. Straight to the point. And she was right. The painting was dead. I had spent an hour embalming it.

I stood there for about ten seconds thinking, okay, now what. Then I grabbed a blue shop towel, put a little Gamsol on it, and started a light wipe-down. Not a full wipe. A working wipe. Pushing and pulling edges that had gotten too hard. Simplifying whole sections that did not need the detail I had given them. Dissolving the fussiness back into something I could work with. And most important, reestablishing the story. Those red umbrellas were the reason I had stopped at this spot in the first place. I had forgotten about them somewhere in the middle of painting bricks. I brought them back.

The entire painting started to breathe again. Within a few minutes, I could see it working, and my mood shifted from dejected dud to a painting that might hold up. I went on to finish it. It sold quickly in the final show.

The lesson is not about the wipe. The lesson is that the wipe was available the whole time, and I could not reach for it until I was told plainly

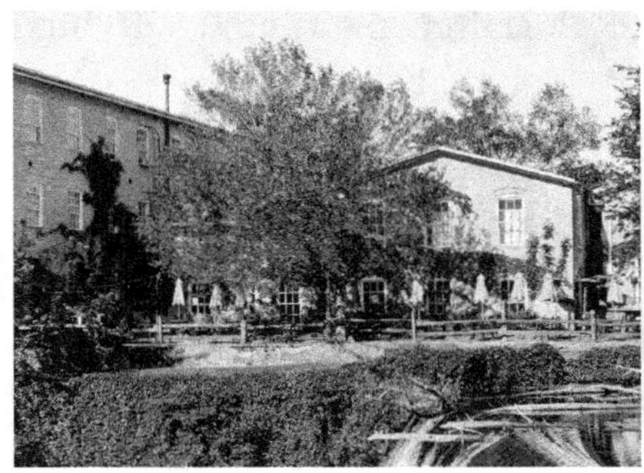 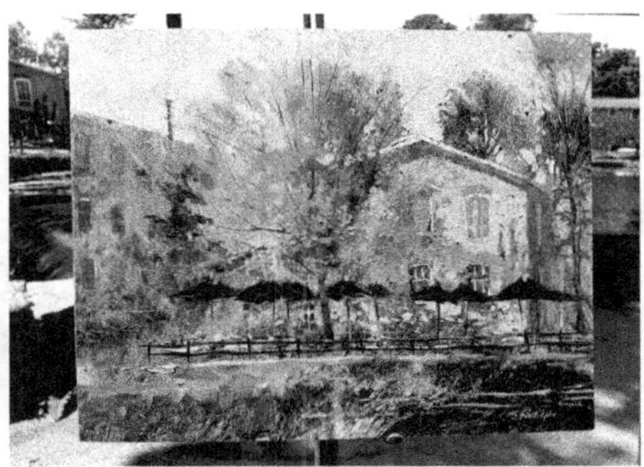

what I already knew. An honest voice at the right moment is worth more than any technique. And the technique, when I finally used it, was not destroying the painting. It was rescuing it by removing what should never have been there in the first place.

"I love her for never wasting her voice on flattery. Straight to the point. And she was right."

The studio problem specific to oil is the cleanup. Solvents, mediums, dirty brushes, palette buildup. Five minutes at the end of every session is the price of admission to oil painting. Skip it twice and you will find yourself with no clean brushes on a day you want to work, and the session will collapse before it starts.

Oil reset in one line: When in doubt, scrape to the ground and restate the big shapes. Or wipe back to the story and let the painting breathe.

Watercolor

Watercolor is the least forgiving medium in one specific way: you cannot cover a mistake without losing the thing that makes watercolor watercolor. The transparency is the whole point. Once you start piling up opaque layers to save a failing passage, you have stopped painting a watercolor and started painting a bad gouache. The medium punishes the rescue.

The reset for a watercolor in trouble is therefore different. You cannot scrape. You cannot wipe. What you can do is start a new one. A quarter sheet or smaller. The failing painting gets set aside, not scraped. You start fresh and reconnect with the medium's transparency. Nine times out of ten, the fresh start is the real fix. The failing painting was trying to become something it could not become on that sheet of paper.

The other reset for watercolor is the shower. This sounds ridiculous and it works. Take the failing painting into the bathroom, put it under the shower head, and wash it. Gently at first, then more firmly if you have the nerve. You will be amazed what comes off and what stays. Sometimes what is left is the painting you were trying to make the whole time, freed from the parts that were not working. Edgar Whitney used to recommend this. So did James Fitzgerald. It is an old trick and it still works.

The studio problem specific to watercolor is paper. Bad paper ruins good painting before the first stroke. Cheap paper absorbs unevenly, buckles, refuses to hold an edge, and turns your washes into mud. If watercolor is your medium, invest in real cotton paper and never apologize for the expense. It is the single most important purchase you will make.

Watercolor reset in one line: When in doubt, start fresh on a smaller sheet, and trust the transparency.

Gouache

Gouache is the middle child. It reactivates when wet, so you can rework it, but it punishes muddy mixing more than any other medium. A gouache painter who is not careful with their palette ends up with chalky, dead paintings that look like ghosts of what they meant to make.

The reset for a gouache painting in trouble is usually a palette reset, not a painting reset. Remix clean piles of color. Start with pure pigment and white. Abandon the dirty mixes that were producing the chalk. Then come back to the painting and repaint the failing passages with clean, bold color. Treat gouache like poster paint, not like watercolor. It rewards opacity and confidence. It punishes timidity.

The studio problem specific to gouache is tube management. Gouache tubes dry out faster than oil or watercolor tubes, especially if the caps are not cleaned and tightened at the end of each session. A dried tube of expensive gouache is a small tragedy that could have been prevented with ten seconds of care. Wipe the threads. Cap tightly. Every time.

Gouache reset in one line: Clean the palette. Mix fresh. Paint boldly.

Acrylic

Acrylic dries fast. That is the defining feature, and everything about an acrylic reset has to work around it. You cannot wipe your way back the way you can with oil. You cannot start fresh on wet paper the way you can with watercolor. Once the paint is down and dry, it is staying there unless you sand it off or paint over it.

The reset for acrylic is therefore preventive, not corrective. The best acrylic painters I know mist their palettes constantly with a spray bottle, use a stay-wet palette, mix larger pools than they think they need, and work with a looseness that accepts the speed of the medium. They do not fight acrylic's dry time. They use it.

When an acrylic painting is in trouble, the most effective reset is to paint directly over the failing areas with fresh opaque color, once they are dry. Acrylic is built for this. The overpainting is not a patch. It is a legitimate technique that the medium rewards. A painting that has been overpainted two or three times often has a depth and a confidence that a single-pass painting lacks.

Acrylic reset in one line: Let it dry, then paint right over it. The medium forgives the boldness, not the hesitation.

Drawing

Drawing is the most direct medium and the most exposed. There is no color to hide behind. There is no underpainting to cover. Every mark is visible, and every mark tells the truth about the state of your hand and your eye on the day you made it.

The reset for drawing is speed. When a drawing is stiff, try drawing faster, looser, and with less reverence. Fill a page with one-minute gestures of the same subject. Ten drawings in ten minutes. By the eighth drawing, the hand has remembered how to move, and the ninth or tenth drawing will have something the first one did not: looseness, confidence, life.

The other reset for drawing is to change the tool. If you have been drawing with a pencil and it feels stiff, switch to a brush pen. If you have been using a brush pen, switch to charcoal. If you have been using charcoal, switch to a ballpoint. A different tool forces a different kind of attention, and the different attention often unlocks what was stuck.

Drawing reset in one line: Draw faster. Ten in ten. Then pick a different tool and do it again.

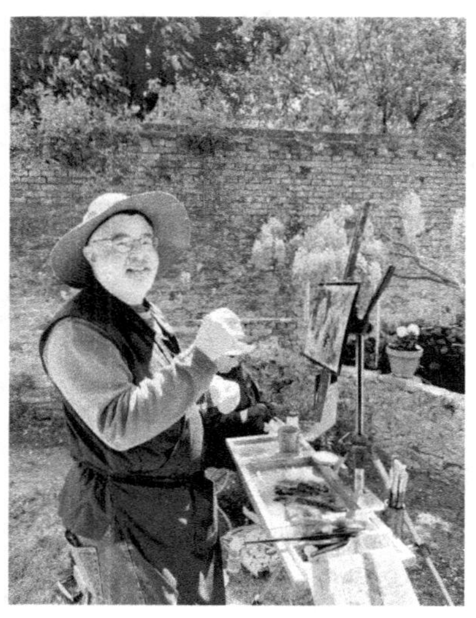

2. Plein Air

Plein air painting is its own country. The rules inside that country are different from the rules of studio work, and the painter who does not understand the difference will lose most of what makes plein air worth doing in the first place.

The fundamental fact of plein air is that the light is moving. Your subject will not hold still. By the time you have set up the easel, committed to the view, mixed the first colors, and started painting, the shadows have already shifted. If you chase the shifting shadows, you will end up with a painting that is half one light effect and half another, and it will look confused because it is confused. You were trying to paint two paintings at once.

The only strategy that works is to commit to one light effect in the first five or ten minutes and paint that, no matter what the sun does afterward. Note where the shadows were when you started. Note the key value relationships. Paint those. When the shadows move, ignore them. You are painting the memory of the first five minutes, not the shifting present.

Here are the other things plein air painters have to manage.

- **The setup tax.** Every minute you spend setting up is a minute you are not painting. Simplify the kit. Streamline the process. A painter who can be painting within five minutes of arriving at a spot has an enormous advantage over one who takes twenty-five minutes to get set up.

- **The site selection problem.** Wandering for forty-five minutes looking for the perfect view is how you lose the morning. Give yourself five minutes to choose. Any spot is paintable. The perfect spot is usually the one you stopped walking at.

- **Scale discipline.** When starting out, do not try to paint a large piece on location. Small formats, eight by ten or smaller, are good. Bigger formats belong in the studio, possibly informed by plein air studies, but not painted entirely from life.

- **The public.** People will stop. They will ask questions. They will tell you about their cousin who paints. Decide in advance how much you will engage. It is fine to be polite and brief. It is not rude to keep painting while you talk.

- **The weather.** Dress for twenty degrees colder than you think you need. Bugs, sun, wind, rain. Be ready. A painter who is shivering is not painting well.

The plein air reset, when a painting on location is not working, is simple and severe: wipe it or scrape it, and start fresh on a new panel. You have probably spent less than an hour on it. The loss is small. The benefit of a clean start, with the lessons of the first attempt fresh in your mind, is large. Plein air painters who cannot let go of failing paintings turn every session into a three-hour rescue operation. Better to make four paintings in a morning, three of which are bad, than to spend the whole morning on one that was doomed by the thirty-minute mark.

Idea: Use plein air as warm-up for studio work, not as a separate discipline. Edgar Payne did this. Scott Christensen does this. The studies made on location feed the larger paintings made later in the studio, and both sides of the practice get stronger for the relationship.

3. The Teaching Artist

If you teach, this section is for you, and you probably need it more than you think.

Teaching is generous, consuming work, and the thing it consumes is the exact energy that painting requires. When you teach a five-day workshop, you spend forty hours demonstrating, explaining, correcting, encouraging, watching, adjusting. At the end of each day, the tank that you would normally bring to your own easel is nearly empty. The idea of going home to paint after teaching all day is, for most of us, a non-starter. So we do not paint. And then the workshop ends, and we promise ourselves we will get back to our own work next week, and next week has its own demands, and the gap stretches.

The problem is not teaching itself. Teaching is a calling for many of us, and the best teaching comes out of working artists who are still making real work. The problem is letting teaching consume so much of the creative energy that the personal work starves. When that happens, the teacher slowly becomes a performer of old lessons, and the freshness that made them a good teacher in the first place starts to fade.

Here are the things I have learned about protecting the painter inside the teacher.

- **Protect one day a week for your own work.** Not one hour. One day. And not the day after a workshop, when you are wrung out. A day earlier in the week, when you still have something to give.

- **Paint without an audience.** Your studio day is not for demonstrations. It is for the kind of painting you would never demo because you do not know how it is going to turn out. Take the risks you cannot take in front of students.

- **Make things that fail.** Your students need you to still be a painter who is discovering, not a teacher who has it figured out. Let some of your personal paintings fail in interesting directions. The failures keep you alive.

- **Separate the voices.** The voice you use in teaching is not the voice you use in your own head at the easel. Learn to switch between them. The teaching voice is explaining. The painting voice is listening.

- **Guard the well.** Teaching draws from the same well as painting. If you do not refill the well, both dry up. Reading, walking, looking at work, going to museums, sitting in silence. These are not optional for a teaching artist. They are the infrastructure.

"Your students need you to stay a painter, not just a teacher. The best teaching comes from an artist who is still making discoveries at the easel, not recycling old ones."

I have taught for many years and will probably teach for many more. A few years ago, I was standing in line at the end of a Paint Cedarburg event, waiting my turn to pick up my art. The line was long, the way it always is after a show, and the artist behind me struck up a conversation. We talked about sales for a few minutes, which is the polite opening, and then we got to the better question, which was how we might paint a little stronger next time.

I told her what I have come to believe about paint carrying emotion from the heart to the brush. If you paint fearfully, you get a fearful painting, whether or not you meant to. If you paint with confidence, the confidence shows up in the strokes themselves, and the viewer can tell, even if they cannot say how. I told her that too many painters confuse detail with depth, that the strength is often in the simplification, and that most artists do not give themselves permission to exaggerate the shapes and colors that would make their work sing.

And then I told her about Eugene Hall.

Mr. Hall was my oil painting instructor at the American Academy of Art in Chicago. He was a man of faith, though he did not often talk about it directly. He did not need to. When you watched him paint his weekly demos in class, his faith was in the brushwork. You could see it in his hand. The way he moved paint around on a panel was a kind of sermon delivered without words. Watching him paint, you knew God existed. That was the effect. You did not need him to say it.

When I finished telling the story, the artist behind me in line looked at me for a long moment and said, "You would make a good priest."

I had heard that sentence exactly once before in my life. My grandmother Molly had said it to me fifty years earlier. I had not thought of it in decades. I told my new friend what my grandmother had said, and she looked at me again and said quietly, "She saw it too."

I am not a priest. I teach painting. But the longer I teach, the more I understand that teaching at its best is close to the same work. You are trying to pass along something you received, without losing it in the passing. You are trying to make a student see what you saw, without insisting they see it your way. You are trying to be, for five days or fifty, the kind of teacher your own best teacher was to you. Hall never lectured me about faith, courage, or humility. He painted, and I watched, and the lessons arrived through the watching. That is the standard I try to hold myself to when I stand in front of my own students.

I do not always meet it. But I remember who set it.

The single most important thing I have learned is this: the teacher who does not protect their own practice becomes, over time, a diminished version of the artist who started teaching. The teacher who does protect it stays current, stays fresh, and brings something real into every class that a purely verbal teacher cannot fake. Your students can tell the difference even if they cannot name it. So can you.

4. Post-Success Stalling

This section will sound like a luxury problem until you have it, at which point it will sound like a life-or-death one.

The pattern goes like this. For years you worked in relative obscurity. You made the paintings you wanted to make, the ones that scared you a little, the ones you were not sure anyone would like. Some of them worked. A gallery noticed. A collector bought a few. You had a good show. You won an award. Suddenly there is an audience. Suddenly the gallery wants more. Suddenly there is a next piece expected, and a piece after that, and a reputation to uphold.

And the painting stalls.

Not because of failure. Because of success. You find yourself second-guessing decisions you used to make in thirty seconds. You worry that the next painting has to be as good as the last one that sold. You stop experimenting, because failure now has an audience. You start painting in the style people bought, instead of the style that got you there. The work, which used to be discovery, becomes protection. And protective painting is rarely good painting.

Here are the things that help.

- **Keep a hidden practice.** Make work that no one will ever see. A sketchbook, a box of studies, a folder on your computer. Make it regularly. The hidden practice is where your voice stays alive.

- **Break your own rules on purpose.** Once a quarter, make a painting that deliberately does not look like your usual work. Wrong subject, wrong palette, wrong scale. Not because you want to change directions. Because you need to remember that you can.

- **Remember who you were before they were watching.** The painter who made the work that got noticed was not yet worried about the audience. That painter is still in there. Protect them.

- **Separate the gallery relationship from the studio relationship.** The gallery is for the finished work. The studio is for the making. Do not let gallery expectations walk into the studio with you.

- **Accept that some paintings will disappoint people.** You cannot be loved into your best work. You will occasionally disappoint collectors, galleries, and even yourself. That is not failure. It is the cost of continuing to grow.

The painters I most admire all seem to handle success by refusing to let it change the part of their practice that made them successful in the first place. They stay experimental. They stay curious. They keep some of the work private. They disappoint their markets occasionally, and they survive it, and the next round of work comes back stronger. The ones who lose this battle produce work that gets technically more polished and emotionally more cautious, year by year, until eventually they are making the same painting over and over with minor variations. Nobody remembers those painters a generation later.

*"You painted before anyone was watching.
You can paint that way again."*

5. The Palette as a Design Problem

Most artists treat the palette as a collection of favorite colors. That is not what a palette is. A palette is a design tool. Every painting decision begins there. If your palette is a mess, every color decision that comes out of it will inherit the mess. If your palette is ordered, every color decision will inherit the order.

Here is what a well-ordered palette does for you. It tells you, at a glance, what is available. It separates the warms from the cools so you are not mixing them by accident. It puts the colors you use most in the positions that require the least reach. It keeps clean mixing zones separate from the pure pigment. It does half the color thinking before you even begin the painting.

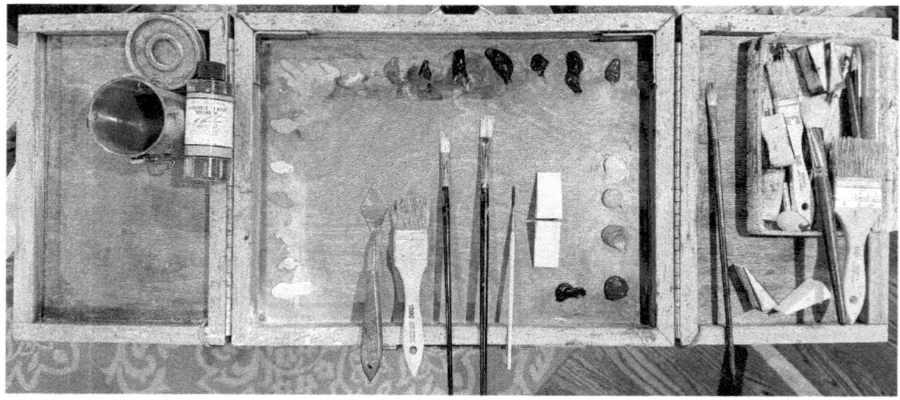

Here's my typical palette layout, Transparent colors at the top, Modifying opaques on both sides.

Here is what a messy palette does. It makes you mix colors on top of yesterday's leftover piles, which contaminates every new mixture. It hides clean pigments under dirty ones. It forces you to hunt for the color you want. It turns every color decision into a wrestling match instead of a direct response to what the painting needs.

The palette reset is simple. Clean it completely. Wipe it down or scrape it flat. Squeeze out only the colors required for the painting you are about to make, in the same position every time. Mix the dominant color families first, in large enough pools to last through the whole painting. Then begin.

If you do this before every session, a week of paintings will show a noticeable improvement in color confidence, and you will not be able to tell me exactly why. The reason is not mysterious. The reason is that you stopped fighting the palette and started working with it.

A Few Palette Practices Worth Trying

- Always squeeze your colors in the same order. Muscle memory is a form of attention.

- Keep warms on one side, cools on the other. Use the middle mixing.

- Try different approaches to your starts until you find your voice. Try a transparent block-in method,

- After a successful block-in Pre-mix three or four color mother pools of paint you'll need to finish.

- Use a larger palette than you think you need. Cramped mixing zones produce cramped color.

- For oil: a glass palette on a neutral-gray surface is worth the investment. You can scrape it clean in thirty seconds.

- For watercolor: a palette with deep wells keeps mixing pools from contaminating each other.

"A messy palette produces messy paintings.
The color decisions inherit the condition they were made in."

---

6. Reference Photography as a Skill Gap

Here is a truth that painters rarely admit to themselves: many of us blame the painting when the real problem is the reference. A flat photograph with poor composition, weak light, and no value structure will produce a flat painting with poor composition, weak light, and no value structure.

The camera cannot design. It records. If you paint what the camera gives you, you inherit whatever the camera missed, which is usually a lot.

Reference photography is a separate skill from painting, and it needs to be practiced separately. A painter who takes good references will make better paintings than a painter of equal skill who takes careless ones. The difference is not the hand. The difference is what the hand is given to work from.

Here is what good reference photography involves.

- **Composing in the viewfinder.** Not pointing and shooting. Really looking at the rectangle and deciding what is inside it. Where is the focal point? What is getting cut off? What is cluttering the edges? Would a step to the left make the shape work better?

- **Shooting for value, not subject.** The camera can lie about color and distance. It is more honest about value structure. When you take a reference, squint at the scene and look for the value pattern. If the pattern is not strong in real life, no camera setting will rescue it.

- **Shooting at the right time of day.** Flat midday light is almost never good reference material. Early morning, late afternoon, and overcast days produce the directional light that makes paintings possible. If you can only shoot at noon, wait for a different day.

- **Shooting many, keeping few.** Take ten shots of the same subject from slightly different positions. Review them later on a larger screen. Keep one. Delete the others. The editing is where most painters fail. They keep everything, and the mediocre references drown the good ones.

- **Painting from Tablets vs Phones vs Monitors.** You can paint from any of them, but they are not equal. I prefer a tablet or a computer monitor over a phone, in that order. Whichever device you use, change the auto-lock setting to "never" before you start painting, so the screen does not go dark on you mid-stroke. Set it back to normal when you are done.

- **Printing the ones that matter.** A reference on a phone screen is not really a reference. It is a glowing rectangle that lies about value. The screen is an additive light source, throwing light directly at your eye. Your paints work the other way, by subtracting light from what hits the surface. The two systems will never agree, no matter how good the screen is. Print your serious references at least six by eight inches and paint from the printed version. Your color decisions will get better the same week.

- **Cropping for design.** Once you have a good reference, crop it ruthlessly. The phone captures too much. The painting needs less. Make the crop before you start the painting, not during it.

The painter who treats reference photography as a separate craft, and gives it real attention, eventually discovers that many of the painting problems they thought they had were really reference problems. The paintings start getting better with no change to the painting skills, because the raw material is finally up to the job.

"A good reference is already half a painting. A bad one is a trap you cannot paint your way out of."

7. Framing, Finishing, and the Presentation Bottleneck

Some painters paint well and never get the work out the door. The unframed paintings stack up. The backlog grows. The artist feels productive because they are making work, but the work is not reaching anyone. It lives in the studio, where it slowly turns into clutter and guilt.

The finishing side of painting is a different job from the making side. That is the root of the problem. Painting is one skill set. Varnishing, framing, photographing, signing, packaging, shipping, and delivering is another. Most of us are drawn to painting and indifferent to finishing. The indifference is understandable. The consequence is that the work never leaves the room.

Here is what has helped the painters I know who have solved this.

- **Build finishing into the workflow, not at the end of it.** When a painting is done, schedule its varnish, photograph, and frame within one week. Do not let it sit waiting for a finishing session that never comes.

- **Batch the tasks.** Frame five paintings at once. Varnish ten at once. Photograph a dozen at once. Batching turns finishing from a chore into a quick session, and one afternoon a month of batching can keep you current.

- **Separate finishing space from painting space.** If you can, designate an area or a different table for finishing work. Psychologically, it helps to not be finishing in the same spot where you paint. The modes are different. The spaces should be too, when possible.

- **Hire out what you can afford to hire.** Custom framing is expensive but a good framer is worth every dollar if it means paintings actually leave your studio. If budget allows, outsource the finishing steps that are the biggest bottleneck for you.

- **Set a clear definition of done.** A painting is not finished when you sign it. A painting is finished when it is varnished, photographed, framed, documented, and either hung, shipped, or stored with its completion date. Until all of that has happened, the painting is still in progress. This definition, once you adopt it, changes how you think about your output.

The painter who masters the finishing side is not a better painter. They are a more complete professional. And their work reaches the world, which is most of the point of making it.

8. Age and Changing Capacity

The painter in their seventies does not have the body of the painter in their thirties. This is not a catastrophe. It is a season change. The question is not whether capacity changes over time. It does. The question is whether the artist adjusts the practice to match the life they have, or keeps trying to run the old practice in a newer body and slowly grinds themselves down.

Here are the changes that typically show up and the adjustments that help.

- **Vision changes.** Reading glasses for close work. A good magnifier for detail. Adjustable lighting that you can aim where you need it. None of this is a sign of defeat. All of it is a sign that you are taking your eye seriously as the instrument it has become.

- **Standing gets harder.** A good adjustable stool at the right height for your easel. A rubber floor mat for the times you do stand. Frequent breaks. Sit and stand in rotation. The body you are painting in is the body that has carried you for decades. Treat it kindly.

- **Long sessions get shorter.** You may have three good hours instead of eight. Those three hours can be extraordinary if they are protected and well-used. The loss of the other five is not a loss of ability. It is a redistribution of energy. Plan around the three good hours rather than mourning the five you do not have.

- **Smaller formats become practical.** Moving large canvases, stretching big surfaces, reaching across wide paintings, all of these get harder. Smaller formats are not a compromise. They are a different scale of ambition, and many of the greatest paintings in history were small.

- **Stamina decisions become strategic.** You cannot paint everything you used to paint. You can still paint the most important things. The question becomes: what is worth the remaining energy? The answer, for most painters in this season, is work that is closer to the bone than ever before.

I have known painters who did their strongest work in their seventies and eighties, not despite the reduced capacity but because of it. The reduction forced them to paint only what mattered most. The result was work with less filler and more essence. Monet painted his last water lilies mostly blind. Matisse made his cutouts from a wheelchair. Andrew Wyeth kept making powerful paintings into his late eighties. Constraints did not stop them. Constraints focused them.

"Adjust the container, not the standard.
Paint smaller if you must, but paint well."

---

9. The Post-Workshop Crash

This one happens to every painter who takes workshops, and almost nobody warns you about it in advance.

You sign up for a workshop with a teacher you admire. You go for four or five days. The setup is perfect. The instruction is clear. The energy of the room is high. You are surrounded by other painters who are all trying hard and being generous with each other. You paint four or five pieces during the week that are, honestly, better than most of what you make at home. You go home inspired, full of new ideas, convinced that something has shifted and that your painting will never be the same.

Within two weeks, the magic is gone. The new paintings look like your old paintings. The lessons feel like they are already slipping away. The workshop pieces look, from this distance, like someone else painted them. You try to replicate the conditions and nothing happens. You start to wonder if the workshop was a kind of illusion, or if you are the one who is broken for not being able to hold onto it.

Here is what is happening. The workshop conditions were artificial. Not in a bad way. Artificial in the sense that they were deliberately designed to remove friction. A perfect setup, curated subjects, constant expert feedback, focused peer energy, and no distractions from home life. Of course your paintings were better. You were painting in optimal conditions that you do not have at home.

The crash is not failure. It is re-entry. You are returning to your normal conditions, and the paintings will reflect the conditions, not the workshop version of you. The workshop was a glimpse of what is possible. Home is where you translate the glimpse into your ordinary practice, which takes time.

Here is what helps.

- **Write down three things within a week.** Not techniques. Principles. The three things you learned that were the biggest shifts for you. Write them in a notebook. Tape them to your easel. Keep them visible for a month.

- **Apply one principle per painting.** Do not try to adopt everything the instructor showed you. Apply one idea, deliberately, to your next five paintings. Then add another. Assimilation is slow. Honor that.

- **Do not try to replicate the workshop paintings.** Those paintings happened in those conditions. Let them be what they were. Your home paintings will be different. That is not a deficiency. That is reality.

- **Give it three months.** The real absorption of a workshop usually shows up two or three months later, in a painting you make that would not have been possible before. Not the next one. The one in June, if you took the workshop in March.

- **Protect the afterglow with a small ritual.** A short session the morning you get home. One painting, in your own studio, in your own voice, before the ordinary week closes back in. A bridge between the workshop and the regular life.

The workshop gave you seeds, not flowers. The flowers grow at home, in your own soil, over many seasons.

10. Busyness as Avoidance

This is the most dangerous problem in the chapter, because it disguises itself as diligence. A painter who is always busy but rarely painting is a painter who has found a way to avoid the studio while looking productive. It is the most respectable form of procrastination, which is what makes it so hard to see in ourselves.

Here is what it looks like. You are ordering supplies. You are organizing your reference folders. You are watching tutorials. You are reading about color theory. You are planning future workshops. You are updating your website. You are building an email list. You are cleaning brushes that did not need cleaning. You are reorganizing your storage. You are researching new panels. You are on social media promoting your work. All of this feels productive. None of it is painting.

Each individual activity is defensible. Taken together, they add up to a practice in which the actual making of paintings has become a minor activity, surrounded by a large ecosystem of painting-adjacent tasks. The artist feels busy, tired at the end of the day, and quietly confused about why so little work is getting made.

The cure is simple and uncomfortable. Ask yourself, at the end of every studio day, one question.

"Did I actually move paint today?"

If the answer is yes, the day counted. If the answer is no, the day did not count as a painting day, no matter what else got accomplished. You might have done useful work. You did not paint. Be honest about the difference. If the answer is no for three days running, the ecosystem has taken over and the painting has been pushed out. You have a busyness problem.

The remedy is also simple. Move paint first, every day, before anything else. Fifteen minutes minimum. Then, if there is time, do the other things. If you always do the other things first, there is never time for painting. If you always paint first, there is always time for the other things, or there is not, and if there is not, it turns out the other things were less important than they seemed.

I have been on both sides of this. I have spent weeks being busy and not painting. I have also spent weeks painting first and letting the busy work take care of itself. The weeks I painted first were always better weeks, without exception. Not just for the paintings. For everything else. Moving paint first changes the shape of the whole day. Everything else gets done anyway, and the day has a center it did not have before.

One more thing, and then the chapter closes. I am a believer in working six days and resting one. Give your mind, body, and soul a day off. Not a day of catching up on errands. Not a day of cleaning brushes and reorganizing the studio. A real day. No painting, no studio chores, no production guilt. Just rest.

This is biblical, and that matters to me. The painters I know who work seven days a week burn out faster, paint stiffer, and lose their wonder sooner than the painters who keep one day clear. The day off is not lost time. It is the day that makes the other six days possible. The hand needs the rest. The eye needs the rest. The soul needs the rest most of all. And the work you make on Monday is better because you did not paint on Sunday.

Exercise: For the next six days, move paint first, every day. Before email, before social media, before planning, before tidying, before anything. Even if it is only fifteen minutes. Then, on the seventh day, rest. Actually rest. At the end of the week, notice how the week felt, how much got made, and how different the rested day was from the days before it.

Questions to Sit With

Pick the questions that match the special cases most relevant to your current situation. Not all of these apply to every painter. The ones that apply will apply strongly.

- Which medium-specific trap am I most vulnerable to right now? What would a fresh approach look like?

- If I paint plein air, am I committing to one light effect, or chasing the shifting light?

- If I teach, am I protecting one day a week for my own painting? What happens to me when I do not?

- Is success changing what I paint? Am I protecting the experimental part of my practice?

- When did I last clean and reorganize my palette? What would a proper palette reset do for my next week?

- Am I taking my reference photography seriously, or treating it as an afterthought?

- How many finished but unframed paintings do I have in the studio right now? What would it take to get them out the door?

- If I am in a changing-capacity season, what have I adjusted, and what am I still fighting that I should accept?

- When I think about my last workshop, am I still chasing the workshop paintings, or translating the lessons?

- Did I actually move paint today?

- Did I truly rest one day a week?

A Closing Thought

The special cases are special only in the sense that the general rules do not quite reach them. They are not unusual. Most working painters will meet at least half of these problems in any given decade, and many will meet most of them.

The reason they are worth their own chapter is that each of them has its own logic, its own internal rules, and its own specific fixes. A general principle about "good studio habits" will not tell you how to reset a failing watercolor, or how to protect your personal work while teaching a five-day workshop, or how to recover from a post-workshop crash, or how to stop letting busyness replace actual painting. Those require specific answers, and the specific answers are what this chapter was for.

If you are in one of these situations right now, return to that section. Read it slowly. Take the one or two ideas that apply to you and put them into practice this week. Leave the rest for when you need them. The chapter is a resource, not a sequence. It will still be here the next time a special case shows up in your life, and another one will. They always do. That is what it means to be a working painter over a long life: the problems keep coming, and they keep being new, and the practice of meeting them with honesty and craft is most of the job.

The other part of the job is what the next chapter is about. The checklists. The distilled, portable, practical versions of everything in the book so far. When you do not have time to reread a chapter, the next chapter is the one to open.

Of the seven ways of adding value, this chapter was mostly about **Cheaper** and **Faster.** Cheaper, in the sense that matters most in a studio: lowering the emotional cost of a mistake, so a watercolor in trouble can be started fresh on a smaller sheet, or a plein air panel can be wiped down and started over without mourning. Faster, in the sense that a clean palette, a printed reference, and a finishing routine that gets paintings out the door are all ways of removing friction between the painter and the work. Cheaper and Faster are not glamorous values. They are the ones working painters depend on over a long career.

"The problems keep coming, and they keep being new. That is what it means to be a working painter over a long life."

CHAPTER EIGHT

The Checklists

The Whole Book, Folded Small

When you are in trouble in the studio, you do not need a book. You need a card on the wall. One sentence that tells you what to do next. A short list you can run through before the frustration takes over. A single question that cuts through the fog.

That is what this chapter is for. Everything in the previous seven chapters, distilled down to what you can use when you need it most. No essays. No stories. No paragraphs of explanation. Just the tools.

Print the ones you need. Tape them where you will see them. Photograph them on your phone. Tear them out if you have to. This chapter is designed to be used hard.

**"A checklist is not a constraint.
It is a gift your calm self leaves for your frustrated self."**

The checklists are organized in the same order as the book: the room, the routine, the mind, the canvas, the life, the source. Plus a few synthesis pages at the end that combine them all. If you remember only one of them, make it the three-question triage on the next page. It is the spine of the whole book.

THE THREE-QUESTION TRIAGE

When Nothing Is Working, Start Here

What is wrong with the room?

Too crowded? Too dark? Too chaotic?

Hard to move? Hard to see? Hard to begin?

What is wrong with the routine?

No plan? No warm-up? Too many choices?

Too much setup? No defined first step?

What is wrong with me today?

Am I tired? Distracted? Afraid? Unprepared?

Answer these three before you reach for anything else.

Most studio problems live inside one of the three.

Four States, Four Fixes

If the problem is with you today, it is almost always one of these four. They look alike from the outside. They are not the same, and the fix for each one is different.

Tired

What it feels like: Your body feels heavy. Even easy tasks feel hard. Your eyes will not focus.

What you need: Sleep, water, food, movement, or a shorter ask. Not discipline.

The fix: Rest today. Come back tomorrow. Tired is not blocked. Tired is tired.

Distracted

What it feels like: You keep switching tasks. You reach for your phone. You circle the work without landing.

What you need: Fewer inputs and one simple target.

The fix: Phone in another room. Door closed. One reference. Twenty-minute timer. Begin.

Afraid

What it feels like: You know what to do and will not do it. You delay. You organize instead of paint.

What you need: Lower stakes. Smaller scale. A container that holds the fear.

The fix: Small panel. Cheap materials. Twenty-minute timer. Permission to make something bad. Begin.

Unprepared

What it feels like: You want to work but cannot find a way in. No reference, no palette, no surface, no plan.

What you need: Setup, not soul-searching.

The fix: Pick one reference. Make a thumbnail. Write the one-sentence intent. Mix the dominant colors. Begin.

THE STUDIO RESET CHECKLIST

For when the room has gone sideways

- ☐ Clear one work surface completely.
- ☐ Wipe it down.
- ☐ Set out only the tools for one painting.
- ☐ Put your phone in another room.
- ☐ Check the lighting. Same color temperature on palette and canvas.
- ☐ Turn unfinished paintings to face the wall.
- ☐ Place your reference where you can see it without turning.
- ☐ Throw away three things you do not need.
- ☐ Open a window if you use solvents.
- ☐ Make the room say "begin."

THE ROUTINE CHECKLIST

The Six-Step Entry Sequence

Every session. In this order. No exceptions.

1. Choose one reference. Commit to it.

2. Write the story in one sentence: "This painting is about ____."

3. Do one thumbnail. Two inches. Ninety seconds. Three values.

4. Set the three values. Check that the thumbnail reads at arm's length.

5. Mix the big color families before you touch the canvas.

6. Begin with the largest shapes. Cover the canvas in five minutes.

If you cannot finish step two, you are not ready to paint.

Go back to the reference.

STARTUP AND SHUTDOWN ROUTINES

A studio session is a container. It has a beginning and an end. Both deserve a small ritual.

Startup Routine

- ☐ Cross the threshold on purpose.
- ☐ Take one breath.
- ☐ Clear the work surface.
- ☐ Set out the palette.
- ☐ Place the reference.
- ☐ Make one thumbnail.
- ☐ Write the one-sentence intent.
- ☐ Set the timer.
- ☐ Begin.

Shutdown Routine

- ☐ Put the brush down when the timer rings.
- ☐ Step back. Look at what you made.
- ☐ Take a photo of the painting if you want a record.
- ☐ Move the wet painting to the drying area.
- ☐ Wipe or scrape the palette.
- ☐ Clean the brushes you used most.
- ☐ Throw away the rags, the tissues, the trash.
- ☐ Reset the work surface.
- ☐ Leave a bookmark for tomorrow: reference, next panel, next sentence.
- ☐ Close the door.

Five minutes of shutdown saves twenty minutes of setup tomorrow.

Your tomorrow-self is counting on you.

THE MENTAL RESET CHECKLIST

For when the mind is the main obstacle

- ☐ Name what is actually wrong. Say it out loud.
- ☐ Drop the expectation. Choose a study, not a masterpiece.
- ☐ Lower the stakes. Smaller surface. Cheaper materials.
- ☐ Stay off your phone.
- ☐ Set a twenty-minute timer. No judgment during the timer.
- ☐ Give yourself permission to make something bad and finish it anyway.
- ☐ Stop comparing. Close the apps. Close the inner judge.
- ☐ Ask what the painting needs, not what your ego needs.
- ☐ Return to curiosity. Remember why you started.
- ☐ Finish the session before you assess yourself.

Motion defeats fear. Thinking about motion does not.

THE ARTISTIC RESET CHECKLIST

For when the painting is failing structurally

- ☐ State the story in one sentence. Can you?
- ☐ Squint from across the room. Can you see three value shapes?
- ☐ Find the biggest shape. Is there a hierarchy, or is everything equal?
- ☐ Pick the focal point. Where is the highest contrast?
- ☐ Decide what to sacrifice. Every area that is not the focal point.
- ☐ Check edges. Hard, medium, soft, lost. Is there variation?
- ☐ Are you painting big shapes to small, or starting with details?
- ☐ Are you interpreting the reference or copying it?
- ☐ Step back every ten minutes.
- ☐ When in doubt, simplify. Remove, do not add.
- ☐ Stop before the painting goes dull.

Design gives clarity. Story gives meaning. Freshness gives life.

THE LIFE CHECKLIST

For the days life is taking more than it gives

- ☐ Tell the truth about your energy. Am I tired or am I avoiding?
- ☐ Check the body. Sleep, water, food, movement.
- ☐ If the tank is empty, shift to maintenance mode. That still counts.
- ☐ Phone in another room. Non-negotiable.
- ☐ Protect the minimum viable session. Fifteen minutes beats zero.
- ☐ Transition ritual before entering the studio. Breath, hand-wash, word.
- ☐ Name the season you are in. Match expectations to the season, not the ideal.
- ☐ Leave a bookmark for tomorrow.
- ☐ Close the door. Walk away. Come back tomorrow.

Some seasons are for painting. Some are for staying a painter.
Both count.

THE SOURCE CHECKLIST

For when the why has gone quiet

- ☐ Sit and look at something for ten minutes. No camera, no sketch, no plan.
- ☐ Take a walk without your phone.
- ☐ Start a session with sixty seconds of gratitude. Specific gratitude. The tools, the hand, the light.
- ☐ Find one small wonder today. Something you would have walked past.
- ☐ Read something that stirs you. Ten minutes. Not a how-to.
- ☐ Try a silent session. No music. No podcast.
- ☐ Reframe: this painting is a witness, not a product.
- ☐ Make something that is for nobody but you.
- ☐ Cross the threshold on purpose. Mark the line between life and studio.
- ☐ Remember why you started. Go back to the earliest moment.

Wonder precedes work. Fix it at the threshold, not the easel.

THE 10-MINUTE RESET

When you only have a little time and the studio is a mess

You have ten minutes. The studio is not ready. You are not sure where to begin. Here is what to do.

1. Clear one square foot of space.

2. Put your phone in another room.

3. Pick up one small panel or sheet.

4. Pick one reference. Any one.

5. Make a thumbnail in three values. Ninety seconds.

6. Write the story in one line.

7. Set a timer for the remaining time.

8. Paint the big shapes only. No details.

9. Stop when the timer rings, even if you are mid-stroke.

10. Reset the surface before you leave.

Ten minutes of real painting beats an hour of almost-painting.

THE FULL-DAY RESET

When the whole studio has gone sideways

Give yourself one full day. By the end of it, the studio will be ready to receive you tomorrow.

Morning: Clear and Sort

1. Remove everything from your main work surface and easel area.
2. Sort supplies into three piles: use often, use sometimes, do not use.
3. Discard or donate the "do not use" pile. Store "sometimes" out of reach.
4. Clean every surface. Floor, table, palette, easel tray.
5. Turn all unfinished paintings to face the wall.

Midday: Set the Zones

1. Establish four zones: work, tools, storage, drying.
2. Place your easel or table in the best light.
3. Set up lighting. Same color temperature on palette and canvas.
4. Prepare five ready-to-go surfaces.
5. Create a brush and palette station.

Afternoon: Write the Rules

1. Write your startup routine on paper. Post it.
2. Write your shutdown routine on paper. Post it.
3. Write three studio rules. Tape them to the wall.
4. Pick three images or quotes for inspiration. No more.

Evening: Christen the Room

1. Make one study in the new setup. No ambition. Just marks.
2. Run through the shutdown routine.
3. Leave a bookmark for tomorrow.
4. Close the door.

Your first goal is not beauty. It is returnability.

Can you walk in tomorrow and begin?

The Top 25 Studio Problems

If you are not sure what is wrong, scan this list.
Somewhere in it is the thing that is currently stopping you.

1. Cluttered, disorganized workspace.
2. No pre-painting plan (thumbnails, value sketch, written intent).
3. Phone and digital distraction.
4. Overworking the painting.
5. Weak or absent value structure.
6. Comparison to other artists.
7. No warm-up or startup ritual.
8. Fear of starting.
9. Too many unfinished paintings visible.
10. Poor or inconsistent lighting.
11. No cleanup or shutdown routine.
12. Copying the photo instead of interpreting.
13. Perfectionism disguised as high standards.
14. Guilt about taking time to paint.
15. No focal point. Equal attention everywhere.
16. Decision fatigue from too many open choices.
17. Muddy color from poor palette management.
18. Working too long without stepping back.
19. No reference editing. Sixty photos, no selection.
20. Identity tied to painting outcomes.
21. Fatigue. Not enough sleep, fuel, or rest.
22. Loss of wonder. Painting feels like a chore.
23. Isolation. No community, no peer feedback.
24. Confusing busyness with progress.
25. Painting for approval instead of truth.

THE 10 UNIVERSAL RESET ACTIONS

If the chapters all blur together, remember these

You have ten minutes. The studio is not ready. You are not sure where to begin. Here is what to do.

1. **Clear the surface.** Wipe it down. Set out only what you need.

2. **Remove distractions.** Phone in another room. Not face down.

3. **Reduce the choices.** One reference. One palette. One intent.

4. **Make three thumbnails.** Two inches. Three values. Pick one.

5. **Write the sentence.** "This painting is about ___."

6. **Start with big shapes.** Cover the canvas in five minutes.

7. **Squint and check values.** If it does not read, simplify.

8. **Set a timer and stop.** Constraints produce clarity.

9. **Tell the truth about your energy.** Maintenance mode still counts.

10. **Clean up before you leave.** The next session begins here.

MY STUDIO RULES

(Fill in your own. Post them on the wall.)

Every working painter I know has a small set of rules they have made for themselves. Not aspirational rules. Actual rules. Things they will do every session without fail. Here are a few of mine as examples. Yours will be different. They should be.

Phone in the other room.

Start with a thumbnail. No exceptions.

Step back every ten minutes.

Stop before it goes dull.

Five minutes of cleanup at the end.

Leave a bookmark for tomorrow.

Write your own. Three to five rules. Specific, doable, non-negotiable. Tape them to the wall where you can see them when you walk in. When you feel the usual confusion, the paper tells you what to do.

Lines Worth Underlining

The phrases from throughout the book that are most worth remembering, repeating, posting, or sharing. Use them as you would a stack of index cards: pull one when you need it.

Design gives clarity. Story gives meaning. Freshness gives life.

The studio is not a shrine. It is a shop. Keep it ready for work.

You are not your last painting. You are your next honest decision.

Motion defeats fear. Thinking about motion does not.

Thirty minutes of real painting beats three hours of thinking about painting.

Wonder precedes work. If you have lost the wonder, you will not fix it at the easel.

Clean up before you leave. The next session begins here.

Start smaller than your fear. Start uglier than your pride.

A messy room makes a heavy mind.

Do not wait to feel ready. Get ready, then begin.

Squint first. Paint second. Step back third. Repeat.

A painting without an opinion is a painting with nothing to say.

Every edge is a decision. Every decision is a chance to tell the viewer what matters.

If you think the painting is done, you are probably already five minutes past done.

Mileage is the whole secret. There is no other secret.

The painter who paints is lighter company than the painter who is silently resentful about not getting to paint.

The life you have is the only life in which you get to paint.

Gratitude is incompatible with the market mind. The two cannot occupy the same mind at the same time.

A painting is not a product. It is a record of what you saw and how you saw it.

The mind names things. The imagination finds meaning.

Did I actually move paint today?

The problems keep coming, and they keep being new. That is what it means to be a working painter over a long life.

Painting is attention shaped by love. Everything else is just craft.

The Seven Ways, One Last Time

Over the last seven chapters, I have tried to point out at the end of each one, which of Sanborn's seven ways of adding value the chapter was mostly about. Here they are together, in the shape the book took.

The Room gave you Faster and Less.

The Routine gave you Faster and Better.

The Mind gave you Fun and Less.

The Canvas gave you Better and Different.

The Life gave you Less and More.

The Source gave you Fun and Different.

The Special Cases gave you Cheaper and Faster.

Look at the pattern. Every one of the seven shows up somewhere in the book. Most of them show up in more than one place. That is because the seven are not separate buckets. They are seven angles on the same work, which is the work of adding value to what you do one day at a time, one small decision at a time, one honest painting after another.

When you walk into the studio tomorrow, you do not have to think about all seven. You only have to ask which one or two the day in front of you is for. Is today a Faster day, where the goal is to remove friction and paint more? Is it a Less day, where the goal is to cut something that has been draining you? Is it a Fun day, where the goal is to remember why you started? The answer will change from morning to morning, and that is part of the point. The framework is a compass, not a map. It tells you which direction to turn. The rest is up to you.

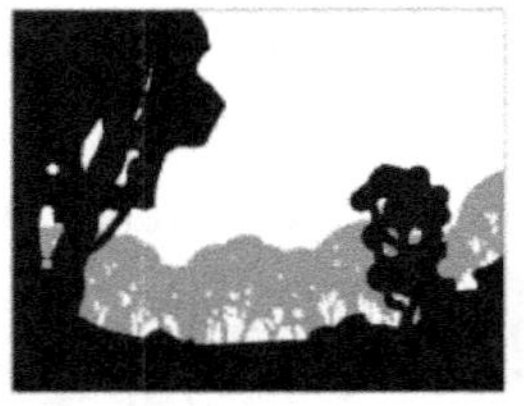
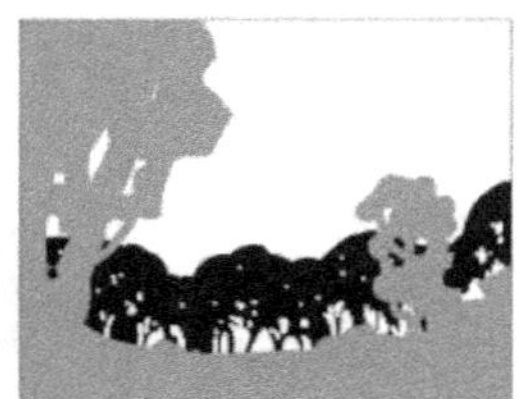
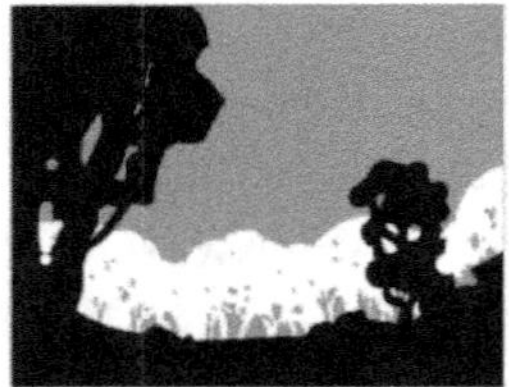
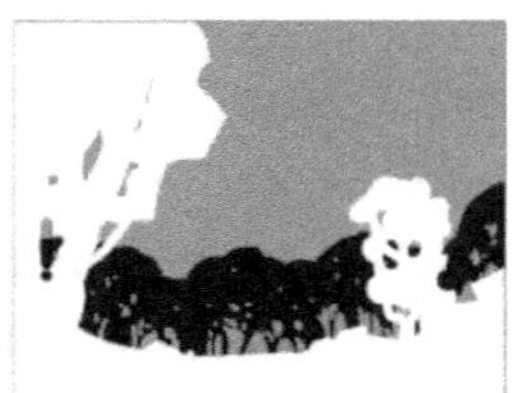
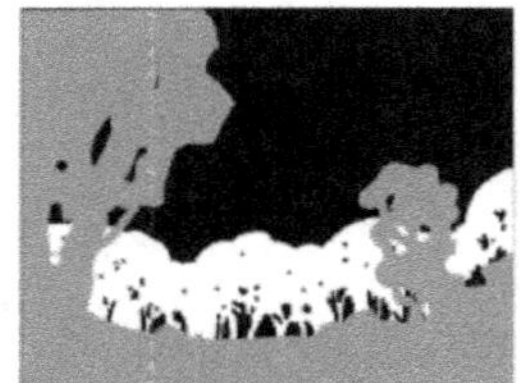
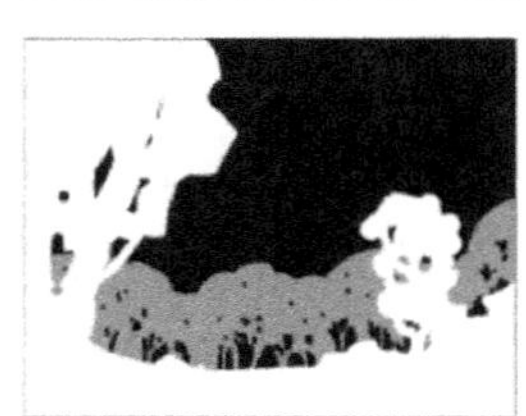

Grounding Your Values

Every one of these six panels contains the same composition. Same trees. Same sky hole. What changes is the assignment — which shape gets the dark, which gets the light, which holds the middle. That's the whole lesson. Before you mix a single color, before you touch brush to panel, you are making a decision that will control everything that follows. These panels are not about rendering. They're about thinking. And they're about one of the most powerful things a painter can do: simplify. Nature doesn't hand you clean shapes. It hands you chaos. Leaves, branches, shadows tangling together into a mess that will defeat you if you try to paint what you see instead of what you know. The artist's superpower is the ability to look at that chaos and say: this is one dark shape. This is one light mass. This is the middle tone that holds them together. These six panels show you what that decision looks like before color happens. Study them. Pick the one that tells the strongest story. Notice how the white shapes read differently depending on what surrounds them. That is not a trick. That is design. When painters struggle and cannot name why a painting went sideways, it is almost always a value decision that went unmade at the start or got made by accident in the middle. Get this right before you open a tube of paint, and the painting will carry its own weight from the first stroke to the last.

A Final Word

You have reached the end of the book. If you have been reading straight through, thank you for the time. If you have been dipping in and out, thank you for that too. The book was meant to be read both ways. Some chapters are for sitting with. Some are for opening in a hurry and closing again five minutes later. This last one is especially built for the hurry.

I wrote this book because I have spent more than half my life walking into studios that were not ready, sitting in front of paintings that were not working, and trying to figure out why. Most of what I learned, I learned from failing. A smaller amount, I learned from teachers who had failed before me and were kind enough to pass along what they found on the way through. The rest I learned from painters I have shared workshops, critiques, and long conversations with over the years. None of this knowledge originated with me. I am just the one passing it on to you.

The book has said a lot of things, but the essential claim is simple. Most studio problems are not talent problems. They are room problems, routine problems, mind problems, canvas problems, life problems, and source problems. All six of those are workable. None of them require you to be more gifted than you already are. They require honesty, consistent actions, and the willingness to keep showing up even when showing up does not feel like it matters.

It matters. Not because any one session matters, but because the sessions stack. The accumulated weight of thousands of ordinary mornings at the easel is what makes a painter. Not the few magical mornings. The ordinary ones. The ones where you did the six-step entry sequence, painted for ninety minutes, cleaned up, and walked out with nothing remarkable to show for it. Those are the days that build the body of work.

When you walk into your studio tomorrow, some of what is in this book will already be there waiting for you, and some of it will not. Take what you need. Leave the rest. Come back for the rest later, when you need it. The checklists are here. The stories are here. The principles are here. They are not going anywhere. You will always be able to find them when the studio goes sideways, which it will, because that is the life.

In the meantime, go paint. Not perfectly. Not triumphantly. Just honestly. Clear one surface. Make one thumbnail. Write the sentence. Cover the canvas in the first five minutes. Step back. Squint. Stop before it goes dull. Clean up before you leave.

Then do it again tomorrow.

"Do the next clear thing. Then paint."

With gratitude for the shared road,

Steve Puttrich

Fairview & Evergreen, LLC

Holland, Michigan

ABOUT THE AUTHOR
Steve Puttrich

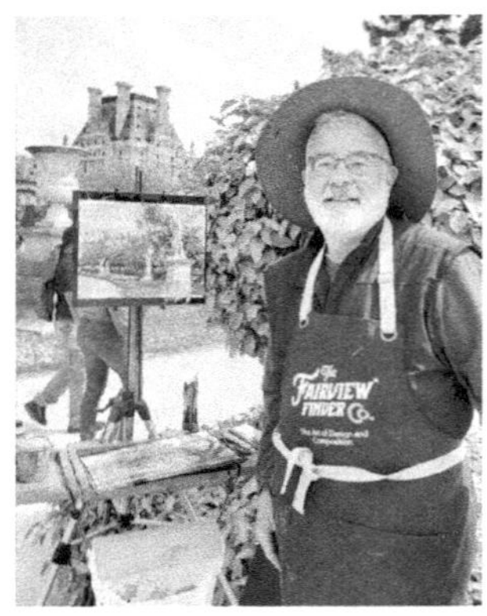

Steve Puttrich is a working fine artist, instructor, and inventor based in Holland, Michigan. He paints in oil, watercolor, and gouache, with a particular love of landscape, plein air, and the portrait. His work has been shown and collected across the country, and his plein air painting has taken him from the shores of Lake Michigan to Apalachicola, Florida, from the Asilomar Pacific Coastline to Fontaine de Vaucluse, France and most places in between.

Steve trained at the American Academy of Art in Chicago and the School of the Art Institute of Chicago, where he learned under teachers whose influence still shapes how he thinks about paint, light, and the craft of seeing. Chief among those was Eugene Hall, the oil painting instructor whose presence is felt throughout this book. Steve credits Hall with teaching him not just how to mix a color or build a composition, but how to carry himself as a working artist over a long life.

Before turning fully to painting and teaching, Steve spent years as an architectural illustrator and creative director at Parsons Corporation, where he learned how design, strategy, and storytelling fit together. That background still shapes the way he teaches painting today. His core teaching framework (Design gives clarity. Story gives meaning. Freshness gives life.) came out of the intersection of his commercial work and his fine art practice. It is the spine of his workshops, his writing, and this book.

Steve teaches oil, watercolor, and plein air workshops nationally, at venues including the Palette and Chisel Academy of Fine Arts in Chicago, the Morton Arboretum, the Chicago Botanic Garden, and private studios and events across the country. He has written for Plein Air Magazine and has been a regular presence in the plein air community for many years, including as an instructor and demonstrator at Plein Air South, PACE and other major events.

He is also the inventor of the Fairview Finder™, a precision composition viewfinder used by painters, photographers, and designers around the world. The Fairview Finder grew out of his own search for a better way to teach composition in his workshops, and has since become the flagship product of Fairview & Evergreen, LLC, his Michigan-based imprint.

Steve's teaching and writing are informed by his Christian faith, which he describes as the source underneath the source. He is married to Bobbie, his wife of more than forty years, and has three grown children: Emilie, Amanda, and John. He paints regularly at Marigold Woods and around the Lake Michigan shoreline. He has been called at various points in his career, a painter, a teacher, an inventor, a writer, and a mentor. He answers to all of them, though his favorite title is still the simplest one: an intriguing shape maker.

"Design gives clarity. Story gives meaning.
Freshness gives life."

Other Work by Steve Puttrich

This book is the first in the Studio Reset series. Future books in the series will go deeper into specific pieces of the painter's practice, including the traveling painter, the teaching artist, the long season, and the daily work of paying attention.

Steve is also the author of the Wonder Walking™ booklet, a short guide to the practice of bringing curiosity and attention to the subjects you paint. Readers of this book will recognize its influence in Chapter Six.

For workshops, books, the Fairview Finder™, and other free and near-free resources, visit:

www.FairviewFinder.com

email: StevePuttrich@FairviewFinder.com

Fairview & Evergreen, LLC
Holland, Michigan

A Note of Thanks

No book is written alone, even if one name goes on the cover. I want to thank Bobbie first, because she has been the honest voice beside me for more than forty years, and because without her, almost none of what I know about painting, marriage, or staying upright over a long life would have come into focus. The red umbrellas in Cedarburg were just one of many times she saved a painting by telling me plainly, and in love, what it needed.

I want to thank Eugene Hall, who is gone now but whose voice I still hear in the studio. If this book has any weight to it, some of the weight is his.

I want to thank the painters I have taught alongside and learned from over the years, at Plein Air South, the Palette and Chisel, the Morton Arboretum, and a hundred other places where working artists gather to sharpen each other. The book is full of things I first heard at a demonstration, a critique, or a late dinner after a long day of painting.

I want to thank Mark Sanborn, whose Seven Ways of Adding Value at Work framework runs through this book like a second spine. Mark granted me gracious permission to adapt his work for the working painter, and I hope this book sends a few of his readers back to his own books, which I recommend without reservation. You can find him at marksanborn.com.

And I want to thank the students who have sat in my workshops, taken my advice seriously, pushed back when I was wrong, and painted through the hard days alongside me. You are the reason the book exists. You are also the reason I keep showing up at the easel myself. We are in this together, and it is the best company I could ask for.

Blessings

Steve

Holland, Michigan, 2026

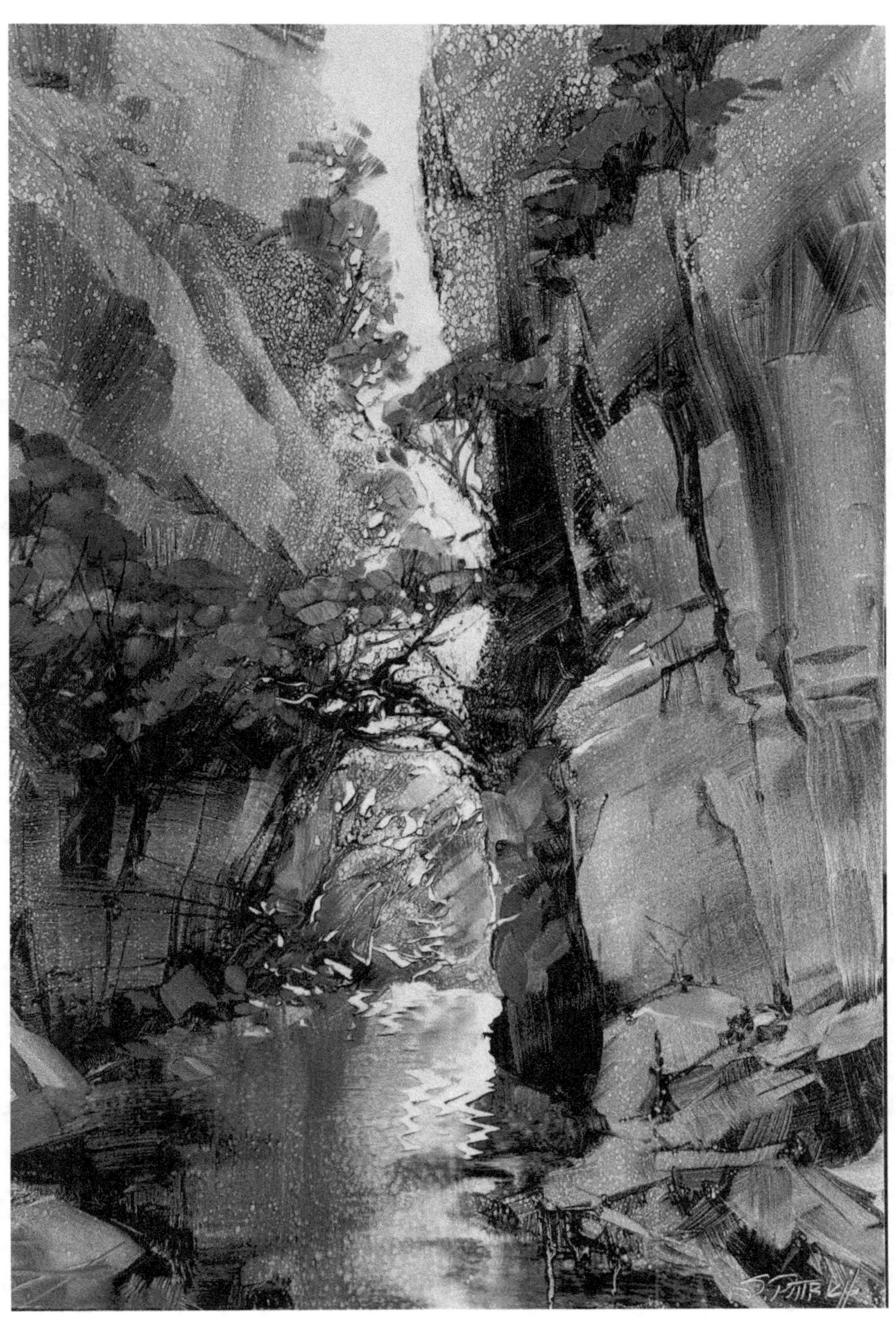

The Passage
Oil on Panel 18" x 12" 2026

www.ingramcontent.com/pod-product-compliance
Lightning Source LLC
Chambersburg PA
CBHW071434130726
47997CB00006B/2084